God Ilens
Steph Skuce
Acts 4:12

Faith Reborn:
Mission in a (Wonderfully) Strange New Ireland

by

Stephen Skuce

cliff
COLLEGE
PUBLISHING

ISBN 978-1-898362-40-1

© 2008 Stephen Skuce
& Cliff College Publishing

British Library Cataloguing in Publication Data.
A catalogue record for this book is available from the British Library.

**Cliff College Publishing,
Calver, Hope Valley, Derbys S32 3XG**

Printed by:

MOORLEY'S Print & Publishing
23 Park Rd., Ilkeston, Derbys DE7 5DA
Tel/Fax: (0115) 932 0643
from data supplied on electronically

Contents

Acknowledgements

Like all authors, I have many people to thank for helping me write this book.

Revds Dudley Cooney, Ruth Jackson and Dr Norman Taggart generously read drafts and provided invaluable insights. Students of mission at Cliff College have stimulated much of the thinking in this work, as have my discussions with colleagues at Cliff College and elsewhere.

As with any writing, I hope that the references in the text and the select bibliography show clearly those whose writing has helped mould my own thought.

Any wisdom in this book is credit to these mentioned and others, the errors remain my own.

Finally, I owe the most to Marlene, Amy and Bethany who make the journey of this life richer than I could ever have imagined.

Introduction

The start of the present century witnessed a plethora of books that critiqued Irish Catholicism. This is not one. Critiques of Irish Christianity in its many varieties form the backdrop to this work but rather than dwelling on the mistakes of the past I am seeking to start to map a very different future. While the deconstruction of Irish Christianity is still necessarily ongoing if we are to truly learn the mistakes of the past in order not to repeat similar in the future, the reconstruction of Irish Christianity is beginning. Yet reconstruction is not the best image as it implies the rebuilding of what was previously there. That is not the thesis of this book. The (re) birth of Irish Christianity as a movement rather than an institution is not certain but is necessary and there are many signs, as this work will demonstrate, that this is what is happening. The urgency of this work is that there is nothing inevitable about this. The mistakes of the past are not automatically learnt and any new forms of developing Christianity are not immune from very quickly falling into the errors of the past (and present).

In order for a positive future to be secured the decline in Irish Christianity needs to be read through the prism of Christendom and now post-Christendom. If not, what is viewed is a local temporary problem that does not need a radical answer. To quote another, there could be an Irish solution to an Irish problem offered, but that would fail to address the main issues. When Irish Christianity is viewed from a post-Christendom perspective a broader picture of the virtual inevitability of present decline emerges. While there are distinct Irish factors that need analysed, the larger view offers a perspective and hope from outside of Ireland. A contextual approach is important but an insular perspective is rarely helpful. There is a very positive future ahead for Christianity in Ireland if it can learn from its own history, from those with a related experience outside of Ireland and engage from the reality of its weakened position to authentically be the community of the disciples of Jesus Christ.

This book is primarily about mission and how Irish Christianity can engage with the emerging culture within which it finds itself. It is hopeful and positive about the future of

Christianity in Ireland, although not about Christendom and institutional Christianity. What this book does is understand Irish Christianity from the perspective of Christendom, and look at Irish Christianity as a whole rather than give a Catholic or Protestant perspective. This twin approach brings a new perception to mission in Ireland, gives a realistic but hopeful assessment of the present and offers a contribution to the future of Christianity in Ireland. The future can never be the same as the past, but is always related to the past, whether for good or ill.

Irish Christianity is currently at a *kairos* moment. The rapid developments in Irish society and Christian institutions mean that the future will be markedly different. Just what that future will be is only now being determined. This book is a contribution to help others think and act in a way that assists the positive, although radically different, future of Christianity.

The mission of Christianity is being re-understood in a very different Ireland. This Ireland might be strange to previous generations but it is wonderfully strange. Developments have opened up many new possibilities and opportunities, as well as brought a number of challenges. However, many of these challenges are prompting Irish Christianity and mission into ultimately very positive directions. If the new Ireland is strange it is wonderfully and positively so.

The South African missiologist David Bosch argued for paradigm shifts in mission thinking as necessary to understand reality. This book calls for an Irish paradigm shift. Christianity has been conceived in institutional terms for most of its 1500 years in Ireland. It might be that the Synod of Whitby, with the triumph of Roman Christianity over Celtic Christianity, was the victory of Christianity as an institution. It may be that it is the twenty first century that sees the necessary rebirth of Christianity as a movement. This may be happening in an unrecognised way already. The recognition and implementation of this may be the paradigm shift needed.

The scope of this book is Ireland – north and south, Protestant and Catholic. Most Irish authors previously have approached the subject of mission in either a denominational or abstract way. This work is deliberately contextual, considering

6

the doing of mission in Ireland by all Christian traditions. Since the Edinburgh missionary conference of 1910, generally recognised as the birthplace of the ecumenical movement, most Protestant denominations have acknowledged their fragmentation to be a missional problem. Since Vatican II Roman Catholicism has increasingly opened itself to outside influence. Each community now recognises that their own constituency does not form the entire Christian community, even if this was a twentieth century discovery. Therefore mission is a common subject and is better undertaken from a broad Christian perspective rather than a narrowly confessional outlook.

That said, my own confessional position is as an Irish Methodist, both by birth and conviction. It may be that one from such a tradition is better placed than most to write such a book as this as I am from a minority faith community yet part of the overwhelming Christian majority. The Methodist faith sits firmly within the evangelical Protestant tradition yet in its founder, John Wesley, has links to many Catholic spiritualities and disciplines. The roots of Methodism are deep and diverse. My family background of a father from west Cork and a mother from Tyrone further helps this broad perspective. My birth was in Mountmellick yet most of my childhood was in Northern Ireland. As a Methodist minister and university teacher I have worked in various parts of rural Northern Ireland, Co Monaghan, Dublin, Sri Lanka and currently England. While we are all captive, to some extent, to our past and present I, like many others, have consciously sought to break out of the stranglehold that tradition can be. This book reflects some of that thinking.

This is not an abstract work but rather one that is earthed in Ireland's specific Christian communities. It is not a book on mission in general, but rather a reflection on mission in Ireland. While it is important to understand missiological principles it is also important to earth this thinking in a specific contextual approach. Ireland north and south is the location. This is more a geographical than political statement. The major Christian denominations organise on an all Ireland basis and individual dioceses, districts, parishes and circuits straddle the border so a study of the doing of mission in the Republic of Ireland or Northern Ireland does not make sense. The distinction is too fuzzy. The recent history of the two parts of Ireland is a related but not shared experience. The Celtic Tiger has been largely the preserve of the Republic of Ireland and while both areas have witnessed significant immigration it follows distinct patterns.

The study of mission or missiology is reflection on the practice of mission. It can never be ivory tower speculation and be authentic missiology. Therefore the first two chapters will offer concrete examples and insights as to how mission needs to be done in the Ireland of today and tomorrow. In Chapter One the recent history of institutional Irish Christianity is reconsidered from the perspective of Christendom. Consequently there is not a narrow reading of Irish Christian 'collapse' but rather a locating of the context within the decline of western Christendom. Chapter Two documents the new Ireland that is now experienced. The changes in Ireland in the last ten or so years have been monumental. This is documented from the perspective of what this means for mission. The various non-Christian faith comm.-unities in Ireland have been discussed in my earlier *The Faiths of Ireland* but what Chapter Three does is look at various competing forms of spirituality in contemporary Ireland, some religious and some not. This is the spiritual background in which Christian mission occurs. Chapter Four considers what is happening within Irish Christianity. While the decline of Catholicism as an institution has been discussed by others, the related challenges facing the Protestant denominations have not been as carefully addressed elsewhere. However, rather than being read as primarily the decline of an institution, *as if that was the whole story,* it is reinterpreted as symptomatic of the rebirth of Christianity as a movement. In Chapter Five contemporary mission values and principles are discussed and in chapters six and seven these values are applied to Ireland to inform missional being and practice. The missional significance of inter-faith Ireland is addressed in Chapter Eight and the final two chapters point to various possible future church communities for Ireland and my own blueprint for the future.

If Irish Christianity is at a crossroads, the direction taken is important. There are currently no obvious signposts. This book is an attempt to help this conversation.

Chapter One:

Goodbye to Ireland's Christendoms

Ireland has many differences from the rest of Europe. Each nation and region has cultural distinctions and the consequences of particular histories form the nation as it is today. But for a small island with a relatively small population part of Ireland's uniqueness in Europe is in having several versions of Christendom.

So, what was Christendom? The designation 'Christendom' is an overarching term to define the period(s) in history when Christian institutions held the prominent place in society, the population formally adhered to an outward expression of belief, normally conformed to a specific lifestyle and where the Christian story was integral to the history and culture of a nation. Many nations have experienced a form or forms of national Christendom but the term can also be used more broadly to describe the culture that emerged, primarily in Europe, from the 'conversion' of Constantine in 312 and his gradual introduction of Christianity as the state religion of his empire, through the many political changes over subsequent centuries through the Middle Ages to the Enlightenment. Nominally Christian rulers enforced Christianity upon their subjects, often as a controlling mechanism, although personal piety cannot be discounted. Christian institutions provided education, health and civil service facilities to the state and in return endowments and a political role and influence for Church leaders enabled the Church to cement its position of privilege. The Reformation in Europe could have challenged this concept but the Reformers, with the notable exception of the Anabaptists, were generally happy to collude with a system that stated the religion of the people was that of their ruler. The continental wars of Reformation Europe bear testimony to this, as do the British, and through geographical proximity, the Irish religious conflicts. Whether the monarch was Catholic or Protestant mattered greatly under Christendom.

Christendom was significantly challenged by the French revolutionaries' call for *'liberté, equalité, fraternité'*. When the

French monarchy fell, to some extent so did the Church and a secular Europe started to emerge. While this has accelerated over the last two hundred years Europe still retains significant aspects of Christendom. Many nations continue to have a national or 'established' church with the United Kingdom a classic example of this. The Church of England is established in law, bishops sit in the House of Lords and there is the requirement for the Head of State to be an Anglican and also fulfil the role of Head of Church. Whilst Germany has no state church much of the population continues to pay a religious state tax of 9% of income to finance social projects as well clergy salaries. Relatively secular Scandinavia retains a similar system.

The initial evangelisation of Ireland enabled a Celtic Christendom to gradually become established when the rulers of Ireland became Christian and it became expedient for the wider population to belong to this new religion. This was a relatively brief flowering, prematurely stunted by the Synod of Whitby in 664 and the official victory of Roman Christianity. Irish faith was transformed and Catholic Ireland was born. This form of Christendom continued unchallenged by the initial intervention of the English in Ireland. English affairs, at least in the passions or political needs of Henry VIII, brought a break with Rome and the formation of Ireland's third version of Christendom. The Anglican established faith, despite never being followed by anything like a majority of Ireland's inhabitants, was a classic form of Christendom. After its formal demise through disestablishment in 1870 two distinct Christendoms developed. Northern Protestant Christendom flourished for a couple of generations after partition while Southern Catholic Christendom lasted a further few years. Ireland is unique as a small island in having had two competing Christendoms with inhabitants of both jurisdictions looking favourably on their own version and suspiciously at the alternative, each view dependant on not much more than birth.

Protestant Christendom

Under English influence, from the sixteenth century the Church of Ireland (CoI) developed as the favoured religious institution. Numbers never afforded the CoI the dominant position that was often the case in other Christendoms but the institutions of state clearly gave a prominence to Anglicans throughout Ireland. The nominal reformation of English Christianity was paralleled, to some extent, in Ireland and Anglicanism was bolstered by the fresh addition of a planted population in the seventeenth century. Of course, not all these newcomers to Ireland were Anglicans. In the north and east, most clearly seen in Co Antrim, the majority of these settlers were Scottish Presbyterians, and even among the English settlers there were Quakers, Independents, Baptists and others that have helped to shape the plural nature of Irish faith. Yet, in most of Ireland, the normal pattern became an Anglican landed gentry supported by an endowed Anglican Church whose clergy provided moral and social legitimacy to the gentry. A small band of loyal Anglican farmers and professionals were supplemented by Presbyterian, and later Methodist, small farmers and shop-keepers. The other Protestant populations, although numerically small, further bolstered the Anglican ascendancy as, whatever the distinctions they considered among themselves, these were usually (but not always) minor compared to the perceived differences with the wider Catholic population.

Pre 1922 Irish society gave a favoured place to Anglicans. In addition to the gentry, the local magistrate and army officers were normally Anglicans and much of the wealth was in Anglican hands. To perpetuate this, early university education, such as at Trinity College Dublin, was reserved for Anglicans alone. Penal Laws were in place to stop the majority Catholic population from gaining more than a foothold in society, with more subtle means employed to maintain Anglican prominence over the other Protestants.

The United Irishmen of 1798 exemplified a shared response by Catholics and Dissenters who understood an Anglican, more than a British, domination of Irish society. Part of the Anglican response was to make overtures to the other Protestant communities to promote a pan Protestant identity. The Orange Order was formed with this Anglican ascendancy motivation of maintaining privilege over Catholics at the expense of including other Protestants in what changed from an Anglican to a Protestant Christendom. Anglican disestablishment in 1870 can

11

be partially understood as widening the Anglican Christendom to include other Protestants so that dominance over Catholics could be maintained, as well as the recognition of the farcical nature of an established faith followed by a small minority.

This form of Christendom continued until 1921 when it came under direct attack. The Irish independence movement targeted this Anglican ascendancy through the burning of many of the 'big houses' where the Anglican landowners maintained their individual versions of Christendom. Apart from the measure of independence gained in 1921-22, the flight of many, but not all, of this elite marked the end of Anglican privilege in the emerging Free State.

In the newly established Northern Ireland it was a different story. The state, as it existed in its six counties form, was a clear expression of Protestant Christendom. The significant Protestant minorities in Donegal, Monaghan and Cavan were abandoned to create a pan Protestant Christendom, although many of these Protestants moved into Northern Ireland through choice or coercion over the next sixty years. This form of Christendom was not a remnant of the Anglican ascendancy that had been lost elsewhere. This new Christendom was a more robust creation under Presbyterian dominance. Many of the other forms of Protestantism incorporated in this Christendom shared the Presbyterian attributes of rugged individualism, frontier spirit and an inherent suspicion of forms of inherited authority.

The era from 1922 to the early 1960s was the highpoint of Protestant Christendom. Brookeborough's 'Protestant Parliament for a Protestant people' was a clear statement of the reality of Christendom. Clergy gave a political lead from the pulpit and in the loyal orders, supporting those Protestants prominent in the police, judiciary, local government, industry and the professions. Exactly when the zenith was reached is hard to determine but a Protestant in Northern Ireland in the 1950s knew that it was 'their' country. Local leaders could be relied on to look after 'their own' and the British leaders, particularly those in the 'Conservative and Unionist Party' remembered the contribution from Protestant Ulster in the two recent world conflicts. Jobs, housing, decent education and a stable society were all guaranteed, as long as you were Protestant. The beginning of the end was when the classic establishment figure, Capt Terence O'Neill, of the Anglican Church, Unionism and the Orange Order, surely someone the loyal Protestants could rely on, started to look south instead of east. Old certainties and assumptions were challenged and the Church-State relationship of mutual legitimation could no longer be guaranteed. The subsequent forty years have witnessed a slow dismantling of the privileged position of the mainstream Protestant churches in Northern Ireland.

Catholic Christendom

A form of Catholic Ireland existed from the nineteenth century onwards, at least on most of the island, due to numerical superiority. The structures of power may still have been in the hands on the Anglican ascendancy but the population of Ireland was Catholic. The surge in church building in the second half of the nineteenth century was testimony to rising wealth and importance. The architecture used was a statement of power and importance and made clear to the rest of Ireland where the faith of the nation lay.

An Irish foreign empire started to develop. In the aftermath of famine mass migration recreated Irish Catholicism abroad, but it was chiefly in the developing USA that an Irish empire was truly established. The eventual success of Irish America financed much of Irish Catholicism in the middle years of the twentieth century.

In 1922 the Irish Free State was a Catholic state and the Church, in a classic Christendom pattern, provided much of the educational, health and social provision for the nation. Recent years have shown that this was not provided perfectly, indeed far from it, but given the context of the emerging Irish state it is maybe unrealistic to have expected much more.

For generations many of Ireland's brightest minds had entered the priesthood and it was this group that considered it their role to provide the religious and moral leadership in both local communities and on a national scale. The priest, school teacher and leading businessmen provided the social cohesion that the rector and landed gentry had provided to Anglican Ireland. In 1937 this Catholic Christendom was reinforced in the 'special place' that the Irish constitution gave to Roman Catholicism, even if this was short of an established faith. This was underpinned as successive governments sought to keep moral laws within the boundaries of Catholic moral teaching. John Charles McQuaid, Archbishop of Dublin from 1940-1971 was rightly described as the 'ruler of Catholic Ireland' and maintained a rigid conservative control on the nation. While the rest of Europe was liberalising its laws on marriage and sexual ethics, Catholic Ireland was still living in the nineteenth century.

This was probably the highpoint of Catholic Ireland. In 1979, when John Paul II visited Ireland, there were already signs of Catholic decline and his visit inadvertently highlighted this. Bishop Casey of Galway, the organiser of the Pope's itinerary and seen on his shoulder in so many of the photographs, was shortly to be exposed as having fathered a child while a bishop and using diocesan funds to deal with the issue. And far worse was to follow. But back in the 1960s Catholic moral authority was supreme. The number of priests and nuns was such that Catholic Ireland was oversubscribed with the large surplus working as missionaries. Catholic Ireland was to continue unto the early 1990s but its days were numbered.

Christendom, in the forms described, has gone and the extent of this decline is now chartered in a number of areas.

Decline of Influence on Politics

The 1937 Irish constitution acknowledged the place and, by default, the role and influence of Catholicism on the state. This continued unabated until the 1980s. Forms of secularism had become established in much of the rest of Western Europe but the Church still dominated Ireland. Church attendance through-out Ireland, and in both Protestant and Catholic traditions, remained high whilst falling in most of the rest of Europe.

While De Valera was a defender of Catholic Christendom he was not anti-Protestant. His Irish Constitution provided a place for minorities, including Jews, but he clearly saw himself as a Catholic politician who sought to create laws in accordance with

Catholic social teaching. The Catholic Church maintained its virtual monopoly of education and national morality was Catholic morality. De Valera's influence on the establishment and development of the Irish state in its first fifty years cannot be overestimated. While De Valera ruled political Ireland, Archbishop McQuaid and others ruled Catholic Ireland and, as a consequence, could be argued as the real power in the land. Laws were Catholic laws and an unofficial veto was held over a significant swath of legislation. De Valera's death in 1975 was one of the markers of the decline of Catholic Christendom.

Other Irish leaders such as John Costello, Sean Lemass, Jack Lynch, Liam Cosgrove and Charles Haughey at least paid lip service to this state-Church relationship, even if not as fulsome in their advocacy of the relationship. As Ireland developed as an independent state it was to be expected that a level of independence from the Church should occur but this was incremental. Whether the present maturity of Ireland was delayed by this close state-Church relationship is hard to determine but it is not coincidental that the present strength of the Irish state has come at the same time as the decline in the institutional Church.

The arrival of Garrett Fitzgerald as Taoiseach in the 1980s brought a new atmosphere. It was not that Fitzgerald directly challenged the existing relationship but his partially Protestant background allowed him a breath of vision not shared by all his predecessors. As an intellectual he had an independence of thought and was not under the spell of the bishops who formed the traditional educational elite in nineteen and twentieth century Ireland. During this era the subservient relationship of state to Church was challenged in a series of referendums. Whilst the Irish population voted to retain traditional Catholic views on abortion and divorce, the significant break was that it was the Irish population themselves who were asked to define moral understanding, rather than politicians who generally acquiesced to Church authority. The Church, officially and unofficially had a significant role in these debates, but it was the people of Ireland, rather than their political or religious leaders, who decided. Independence was finally arriving.

One of the crucial incidents was the rape and subsequent pregnancy of a 14 year old child in 1992. Her parents arranged for an abortion in England and just before travelling contacted the Garda Síochána to see whether any DNA material from the aborted foetus should be retained to assist in any prosecution of the rapist. The upshot was that the full legal and moral force of Irish Christendom descended on the raped child with condemnation of a potential abortion. An injunction forbidding the child the right to travel was sought by the Attorney-General Harold Whelehan and granted by Mr Justice Costello in the High Court. The victim of rape had become the victim of the Irish legal and moral system. The outcome was that the Irish population approved two amendments to the Constitution that, while continuing to keep abortion illegal within Ireland, allowed the right to travel beyond Ireland for an abortion and for information to be distributed within Ireland giving information on how this might be possible. The child in question subsequently miscarried before an abortion could be performed. In this case the Irish population rejected the moral lead of the Church that condemned abortion in all circumstances and sought to overturn the laws that enshrined this moral stance in the state. Morality was no longer to be determined by the Church alone.

The surprise election of Mary Robinson as President in 1992 invigorated an almost moribund post. She was the first President of Ireland elected without the support of Fianna Fáil and her diverse family background contained Anglicans and a judge knighted by Queen Elizabeth II. Robinson had attended Trinity College Dublin in an era when Catholic students were strongly discouraged from attending by the Catholic Church and her marriage to a Protestant further distanced her from the typical model of Irish politician, as did a political career that included campaigning for the easy availability of contraception in Ireland and homosexual rights, both issues strongly opposed by the Catholic hierarchy. Robinson's election was another example of the crumbling of Christendom. The Irish people elected someone who, while a Catholic, disagreed with much of the Church's moral agenda and supported the freedom of individuals to live by their own conscience rather than under an imposed morality. That said, Robinson had a good relationship with the Catholic Church whilst president. Apart from regularly visiting Irish clergy abroad she had an audience in Rome with Pope John Paul II and was the first president to host an official reception for the Christian Brothers.

Bertie Aherne came from a more traditional Irish Catholic background than Robinson and is a regular mass goer. Yet his long reign as Taoiseach has been a challenge to Church influence on politics through his private life as much as anything else. Aherne separated from his wife in 1992 and subsequently had a long-term relationship with Celia Larkin. Ms Larkin's accompanying Aherne on official state business was always a problem to the Catholic hierarchy and at times Cardinal Connell sought to avoid publicly recognising the role of Ms Larkin. That the Taoiseach should provide a 'good' moral example to the population was a preoccupation of the hierarchy but not to the Irish population. Aherne's political career was only very latterly harmed by his private life and he exhibited a robust ability to survive personal financial questions. Indeed, the Irish have shown themselves very ready to forgive, or at least ignore, the indiscretions of their political elite. Once more a censorious Church attitude has not been replicated in the wider population. Aherne's response to the numerous scandals affecting the Church, and their legal implications, has been relatively generous in protecting the Church from economic collapse. But a change is obvious. In former generations the Church provided legitimacy to politicians. In the twenty first century the state is able to hold the Church in a subservient position.

During the various episodes of political violence in recent Irish history the Catholic Church has given vocal opposition to the IRA and Sinn Féin. There have been many instances of individual priests being supportive of IRA activities but the hierarchy has retained a critique of militant republicanism. Despite this Sinn Féin gained considerable political support, especially in Northern Ireland over recent years where the peace process has softened its image. Pope John Paul II's appeal at Drogheda in 1979 went unheeded. The Irish population does not vote the way its religious leaders wish it to do. The Christendom era, where political power was religiously legitimated, has ended.

This Irish Catholic Christendom experience was replicated, to some extent, in Northern Ireland, albeit with a Protestant version. In pre-independence Ireland the Anglican Church gave a measure of religious legitimation to the colonial state but an Established Church, to which a minority of the population belonged, could never have the broad public influence normally enjoyed by a state religion. Post independence Protestants in the Republic of Ireland 'kept their heads down'. Few took an active involvement in politics and those that did rarely drew attention to their Protestant heritage. The community turned inward and sought to maintain its structures in education and health and attempt to live as a state within a state. The significant Protestant communities in the border counties declined through migration to the north and east but the community as a whole was vulnerable. The well-documented economic boycott of Protestant business in Fethard-on-Sea was paralleled with less well-publicised boycotts in the midlands and elsewhere. Protestant Ireland was in the north only. It is significant that near the end of the twentieth century, when there was little elected Protestant representation in the Dáil or Seanad, there were three Jewish TDs representing the three major parties, these Jewish politicians coming from a tiny religious community. Protestant involvement in national politics outside of the north virtually ceased within a few years of Independence.

The nature of Protestantism does not engender a spirit of acquiescence to religious leaders. Dissent and protest is characteristic of the Protestant spirit and so it is to be expected that a Northern Irish Protestant Christendom would be noticeably different to an Irish Catholic version. Yet Protestant-ism does encourage versions of Christendom. The Reformers were often very politically active and Calvinism lends itself to a state-religion engagement. In Ireland individual clergy have had a significant community influence in a related way as to how the Reformers, through force or argument, swayed and galvanised opinion. In 1912 Protestant denominations were active support-ers of the 'Solemn League and Covenant' in opposition to 'Home Rule' but it was primarily local clergy who provided the major influence. Over the years many have contested political office

18

and recent Westminster MPs have included Revds Ian Paisley, Martin Smyth, William McCrea and Robert Bradford. The role of Paisley is the best known and provides, on a grand scale, part of the Ulster Protestant version of Christendom. At his zenith Paisley was able to almost single handed influence Ulster politics in whatever way he chose. His first calling was as a religious leader and part of this vocation was lived out in the political arena. Robust, confrontational, even aggressive religion easily translated to a similar political approach. Ulster Protestants have shown a tendency to respond to clear leadership and this has often been offered by local clergy. Within the Democratic Unionist Party (DUP) there is a clear association between a candidate's declared religious beliefs and its political manifesto. Not all DUP politicians are members of the Free Presbyterian Church, but membership of at least a similar conservative Protestant denomination is expected.

The Orange Order is a fascinating mix of politics and religion. No local lodge is complete without a chaplain offering religious legitimation. Historically it was the local Anglican and Presbyterian clergy, with the occasional Methodist, who filled this office. Today it is more likely to be a lay church member. The Protestant church hall and Protestant school, controlled by clergy, allied with the Orange Hall, were the foci of Protestant communities for generations, and still are to some extent in rural areas. No community event was complete without a grace or opening prayer from a local cleric sitting on the platform. It was a church dominated, if not totally controlled society. This has changed. The role of the Order has diminished and its direct relationship to the Official Unionist Party was recently ended. Clergy are less directly involved in party politics and, while issues of faith are still significant, a direct church involvement is less likely. Ian Paisley's appointment as First Minister with a Sinn Fein deputy caused strains within the Free Presbyterian Church. Paisley's response was to hold on to political rather than religious office, even if that could not be sustained.

The role of Drum Cree should not be underestimated as a pointer to the decline of Church influence in politics. The imagery of Orangemen and others, facing the RUC against the backdrop of a rural Anglican church, did not sit well with many.

The early considerable role of Revd William Bingham as an advocate for the protest changed and by the latter years of the protest there was no significant clerical support from Ireland's mainstream Protestant denominations. What became apparent was the impotence of these denominations to influence events. Despite statements from Church leaders, notably by Archbishop Robin Eames, advocating compromise and extensive 'behind the scenes' facilitation of discussions, the unfolding of events was not significantly affected by these denominations. In 1974 individual clergy, such as Revd Eric Gallagher, had been influential in mitigating the extremes of communal protest that brought down the power-sharing executive. A generation later this was no longer possible.

The DUP provided Northern Ireland's two clerical MPs in 2008, in Paisley and McCrea. Both are in the elder statesman category and Northern Ireland could soon be in the unusual position for the province in having no clergy as senior political representatives.

The main Protestant denominations have consistently advocated forms of power-sharing, supported such initiatives and encouraged members to act accordingly. While not suggesting how an individual might vote, there has been advice as to what principles might guide such a choice. The recent trend to more extreme political representation, example in the decline of the OUP, the SDLP, and virtual disappearance of the Alliance Party, is a pointer that while these Protestant denominations might influence their own core membership, they no longer have the Christendom influence over the wider population. The Church's inability, along with others, to stop the violence in Northern Ireland has been part of the process of secularisation and dismantling of Christendom. When the Church was supporting the ruling powers and justifying robust approaches, it had a voice and significance. When the Church attempted to be more consistent with the Christian message of forgiveness, it found itself talking only to its own members and relegated to the fringes.

Yet there is still a reasonably significant role for the Church and clergy in Northern Ireland. They still can act as community figurehead spokespeople, for example the action of Fr Aidan

Troy in relation to the blockade of Holy Cross Girls' Primary School in north Belfast at the start of the twenty-first century. In 2005 Fr Alec Reid and Revd Harold Good were the 'responsible individuals' asked to witness the comprehensive act of IRA decommissioning. Clergy and the Church still have an important role in Northern Irish political society, but the dominant Christendom influence has gone.

Decline of Influence on Morality

The Church has generally considered itself to be the custodian of the nation's morality and under Christendom the standard of morality for Ireland for 1500 years has been a form of Christian morality. Within Protestant and Catholic Christendoms there have been differences but there has been an agreed overall morality that became enshrined in legislation. But no official system of morality could ever survive the accusation that the custodians of that morality ie the Church and its clergy, failed to meet their own standards. This has become painfully apparent in Ireland over the past fifteen years and has been a major factor in the collapse of Christendom, especially in the Republic of Ireland.

The first publicly significant blow occurred as late as 1992 when it became apparent that Bp Eamon Casey of Galway had fathered a child whilst a bishop and used Church funds to help finance this child. Casey subsequently resigned and moved to a missionary post in Ecuador. Shocking though this was to Catholic Ireland, this incident palls when compared to subsequent revelations. Casey's return to Ireland in 2006 to live in retirement in his former diocese is an indication of the lessening of moral outrage at his actions, at least when seen in relation to other moral failings by Catholic clergy.

The collapse of Catholic Ireland was hastened by revelations of a very significant number of abuse cases and awareness of how the Catholic Church dealt, or rather failed to deal, with the issue. In numerous dioceses, parishes, schools and institutions allegations of physical and/or sexual abuse have been substantiated. Apart from the horror of these crimes and the suffering of the victims, the Church's response, when it became aware of problems, was too often to move the offending cleric to other duties and not report criminal acts to the police. The problem was perpetuated and indeed spread by this action. Institutional collusion and an attempt to protect many of the clergy involved added to a terrible situation and resulted in a virtual abuse of the faith of Ireland. The numerous high profile cases are well known and include the resignation of Bp Brendan Comiskey of Ferns diocese, Fr Séan Fortune, Monsignor Michaél Ledwith of May-nooth Seminary, Fr Brendan Smyth and Fr Jim Grennan. Even the Sisters of the 'Magdalene Laundries' were involved.

While this issue has been largely a Catholic problem it has not been confined to Catholicism with recent resignations for moral indiscretions including an Anglican bishop and a former Methodist president. Institutional Christianity, far beyond Catholicism, has been one of the many victims of this issue. It is an international issue with similar situations in many nations, especially in the USA where the Catholic Church has paid several hundred million dollars in settlements. Also the issues are not confined to Christianity. Buddhism, with a tradition of celibate clergy, has suffered in similar ways in countries such as Sri Lanka.

Nothing can excuse the Irish abuse. When the Church undertook the care of children for the state, this placed the Church in a potentially vulnerable position. Similar problems were experienced elsewhere but Christendom afforded a certain measure of protection to the Church. Whether the decline of Christendom led to the opening up of the abuse issues or whether the abuse issues were a major factor in the decline of Christendom is hard to determine. This said, the involvement of clergy in cases of child abuse is numerically far lower than, for instance, the involvement of relatives. The impression has been given in Ireland latterly that abuse was/is primarily carried out by clergy. This is hugely inaccurate. The role of clergy in child abuse should never be minimised but nor should it be exaggerated allowing other types of perpetrator to escape scrutiny.

The referendum results referred to earlier point to the decline of Church influence on national morality. A similar lack of influence has been witnessed in political morality. Charles Haughey, Liam Lawlor, Ray Burke, George Redmond, Michael Lowry, Denis Foley and Ben Dunne are names familiar to a generation of Irish people. The Flood/Mahon and Moriarty Tribunals have made many lawyers wealthy and highlighted the lack of morality within much of the Irish political elite. Given the close relationship between Church and state in Christendom, Church awareness, and even involvement at some level, in these scandals is hard to refute.

Despite Church opposition contraception became available in the Republic of Ireland in the late 1970s and widely accessible from 1992, censorship declined and divorce became legal after a referendum in 1995. These were battles for public morality that the Church lost. By 2002 almost one third of births in the Republic of Ireland were outside of marriage with the proportion higher in Northern Ireland. The percentage of the population living together outside of marriage is close to other European averages even if openly homosexual couples are still unusual.

Ireland, despite being declared by the *Economist Magazine* in 2004 as 'the best place to live in the world', has become a society where drug use and organised crime is endemic. Parts of north Dublin and Limerick in particular have the reputation of being in the control of gangs while the former terrorist organisations in Northern Ireland have used the peace process to switch their main attention to crime. Not exactly a land where the faith of the people dominates all aspects of life.

Decline of Influence on Education

Education has been a Christendom issue under which the Church provided the educational needs of the nation, and latterly has sought to maintain the privilege of influence over each generation that this brought. India is a current example where a very small Christian community has a disproportionate involvement in education and seeks to maintain that role as a way to influence a wider constituency. For much of Ireland's history Church influence over education was virtually complete. To underline this Church - state allegiance, from 1943-44 the Northern Irish minister for Education was a Presbyterian cleric.

In Northern Ireland education was provided by denominations primarily for children from that denomination. This continued until the 1960s when Protestant schools were handed over to the state in return for rights over governance. The Catholic schools did not join this scheme and while almost all expenses are covered by the state there is still a distinct Catholic maintained system. In 1964 Terence O'Neill became the first Northern Irish premier to visit a Catholic school. Teacher training has followed a similar path from Church provision to being part of the state third level educational sector.

The integrated education movement, whereby Protestant and Catholic children are educated together in a non-denominational setting, gained prominence in Northern Ireland with the opening of Lagan College in 1981. Today most towns have a Catholic school, a state school and an integrated school. Some of the integrated schools have emerged from government refusal to fund a state school with declining numbers but when that school became integrated significant financial funding previously unavailable was able to be found. The Catholic Church in particular has struggled to accept the integrated education movement. In a number of cases, where there is a greater number of Catholic children in an integrated school, one of the motivations has been the desire by nominally Catholic parents to have their children educated in a religiously neutral atmosphere. This is a direct attack on Christendom and all it stands for.

An alternative perspective is seen in the development of a small independent Christian school movement sponsored by the Free Presbyterian Church among others. While much smaller than the integrated education movement this reflects a desire by conservative Christian parents to withdraw their children from the state educational system and place them under the influence of a confessing religious movement. This harkens back, to some extent, to the establishment of denominational education in Ireland but owes most allegiance to a similar movement in the USA that is primarily a reaction against modernity and the teaching of religion as a subject rather than a belief system to be accepted. Not every force is pointing to the demise of Christendom.

The Republic of Ireland has had a similar history to Northern Ireland of Church provision of education that developed into a state system that supported denominational control of schools with the state paying most, but not all, of the costs involved. One further development is the decline in faith commitment of teachers in the Catholic school sector. In previous generations the teacher, educated and employed in a Catholic system, was one of the chief planks in propagating the Catholic ethos and maintaining Christendom. Sacramental preparation occurred in the school and the link between school and parish was clear and strong. This is collapsing due, to some extent, to the lowering level of faith commitment found among teachers. This aspect of Christendom is disintegrating from within but results in interesting mission opportunities and challenges that will be considered in later chapters.

One of the implications of this decline was revealed in a 2007 survey conducted by the Irish Evangelical Alliance. A survey of religious knowledge in the general population showed that those in the 'over 65s' segment had very good scriptural knowledge and awareness of basic Christian concepts. The figures were radically different for the '15-24' segment. Two thirds of the older group correctly identified the Catholic Church as having seven sacraments compared to only one third of the younger group. A third of the older group accurately described the meaning of the immaculate conception compared to a tenth of the younger group. Almost half of the older group remembered the first commandment while only one twentieth of the younger group was successful. What could be taken for granted under Christendom is increasingly no longer the case.

Decline of Influence on Health

The high point of Christendom in health issues in the Republic of Ireland was in 1951 with the Catholic Church opposition to the Heath Minister, Dr Noel Browne, and his Mother and Child Bill. At this time the Catholic Church had a virtual monopoly over health care through its provision of hospital services, but Browne, influenced to some extent by the heath reforms in Britain, sought to introduce a scheme whereby the state would be responsible for maternity provision and provide free health care for all children up to the age of sixteen. This relatively mild proposal was strongly opposed by the Church who saw this as state interference in an area of Church dominance, to increase the possibility of artificial birth control and abortion, and take away from individual families the right to provide for their children. The issue was not helped by Browne's lack of support from his cabinet colleagues and Archbishop McQuaid's opinion that this proposed legislation was contrary to Catholic social teaching. This opposition resulted in Browne's resignation. Christendom's domination over health issues in the political realm was at its zenith.

Since then there has been a gradual, if partial, erosion of Catholic values in healthcare. Browne's basic proposals have been in place for more than a generation and each referendum and decade appears to further distance state legislation and provision from official Church teaching. Today Catholic opposition to a particular health issue is one voice among many, but no longer the dominant voice. The Church can no longer bully the state.

Recent years have witnessed the decline of Protestant influence in health care in the Republic of Ireland. The Adelaide Hospital was the chief centre of Protestant health care and health education, with Barrington's Hospital (Limerick) and the Victoria Hospital (Cork) also important. The Adelaide Hospital merged with the Meath Hospital and when the combined hospital relocated to Tallaght in 1998 six board members of the new hospital reflected this Protestant background and provided an opportunity for Protestant nurses to train in a supportive environment. In recent years the Tallaght Hospital, with a children's speciality, appears to have been overlooked in some health initiatives and there are Protestant fears that this last hold on health provision is being eroded. In reality this is probably the case and is to be expected given the decline of Christendom. A privileged position for a particular religious community was part of Christendom. With its demise, or at least substantial decline, such privileges are lost and Tallaght hospital stands as testimony to this.

Decline of Influence in Community

In a previous generation community leadership in Northern Ireland was provided by clergy supported by co-religionists of the same outlook in the professions. The cleric, the doctor, the lawyer and the teacher, supported by the local sergeant, provided community cohesion. These individuals were the educated people of influence. The local landowners or gentry, who were the traditional political representatives, were often more English orientated and at times took little local involvement. Their children were educated in England, marriage partners were found there and their outlook was eastwards.

Recent generations have witnessed the rise of widespread third level education eroding the position of clergy, among others, as the educated elite of a community. The Church was never very enthusiastic or successful in defending the rights of ordinary people and increasingly lost out to others in providing the needs of the population. Relegated to the provision of rites of passage, and increasingly bypassed for those today, the traditional custodians have been reduced in influence.

Today community leaders are increasingly found among local business people. In rural areas large farmers and shop keepers have risen in influence although the 1990s witnessed the demise of many independent retailers who sold out to British or European multi-nationals. The Celtic Tiger has produced significant Irish business people who are now major economic figures in Britain and abroad. The economic clout of Michael O'Leary among others is such that the state has to listen, whether it wants to or not. If Christendom has gone, it may have been replaced in part by a finance driven power.

In the cities the influence of organised crime has become significant and shows no signs of being on the wane. In the Northern Irish conflict paramilitary groups portrayed themselves as community guardians, and there was a measure of truth to this claim in the 1970s. As community changed so did the role of these organisations from allegedly protecting community to exploiting community through protection rackets, drug trafficking and a form of policing. The ubiquitous kneecapping was more about social domination than community protection.

Community events in Ireland may still include clergy but do not need clergy to legitimate them. In rural areas clergy may still be prominent, but the crucial change is that they are no longer essential. In the cities the public role of clergy in communities has declined with their function mostly confined to advocacy on behalf of the poor and disadvantaged. The Church is increasingly active in raising issues related to poverty, injustice and the position on immigrants, this last role an interesting reversal of the traditional Church role in assisting Irish migrants in their new countries. The decline in vocations, caused as much by the increasing wealth of Ireland and employment opportunities as by religious factors, is not yet a significant consideration in this decline in community significance. Although clergy are aging, Ireland still has a high ratio of clergy to the faith community when compared to much of Europe, although it is to be expected that a decline in clergy numbers in the future will exacerbate this withdrawal from a public role.

Christendom is at least going if not already gone in Ireland. This is not unique to Ireland. Indeed it is Ireland belatedly falling in line with much of the rest of Europe. While there are particular Irish events that are significant, the decline of Christendom, when viewed from a broader European perspective, is inevitable in contemporary plural democracies. This is not a trend that can be stopped, nor should it. Christians can hearken back to 'the good old days', or at least a mythical memory, or they can embrace the new reality. The possibility that the decline of Christendom is allowing the Church to fulfil a more overtly Christian role and enabling the Church to escape from the institution of Christendom and become the movement of the followers of Jesus forms the substance of much of the rest of this book.

Questions

1 Overall, is Christendom a problem to be escaped from or a passing legacy to mourn?
2 Were the good old days actually good?
3 What are the issues for your church in the passing of Christendom?

Chapter Two:

Post-Everything:
A Wonderfully Strange New Ireland

The decline of Christendom is not the only change that Ireland has recently experienced. Several developments have simultaneously occurred resulting in a contemporary Ireland that bears little recognition to that of just a generation ago. The Ireland of the past is not the Ireland of the present and it is the present Ireland in which mission is lived out by Christians. Before a missional understanding can be developed a recognition and appreciation of these changes is necessary. Mission never occurs in a vacuum. If those seeking to engage in mission follow a redundant perspective of Ireland, then it is unlikely that such a missional engagement will be particularly productive. Recognising Ireland as it is, not what it was, or even what we might like it to be is an essential task of an authentic missional engagement. A mapping of how Ireland has changed and its current ethos is necessary to accurately read the new Ireland.

Post-Christian

Ireland is not post-Christian in the sense that Christianity has disappeared. That is clearly not the case. Churches and Church institutions are still important features of individual and community life. But Ireland is post-Christian in that Christianity has lost its dominant, indeed exclusive position. In the Republic of Ireland, while Catholicism is still the nominal religious home of the large majority, the historic Protestant denominations have reversed seventy years of post-independence decline. Today a couple from a Protestant and Catholic background are more likely to raise any children in at least a nominally Protestant way. Irish 'superstars' such as Bono and Graham Norton come from a Protestant background and 'Republic of Ireland equals Catholic' is no longer accurate. In a parallel way Northern Ireland no longer has a dominant Protestant majority. For a generation there have been more Catholic than Protestant school goers and while there is still a nominally Protestant majority the next couple of generations should witness a historic change.

Of greater note is the relatively recent arrival of significant other faith communities in Ireland that is discussed at length in my *The Faiths of Ireland* (Dublin: Columba, 2006). This has already changed the social landscape of Ireland and this impact will continue to increase for the next number of years.

Ireland has had a fascinating history of involvement with people of non-Christian faiths. There are a number of legends that link Ireland with Judaism, for example it is argued that Noah had a daughter who built her own ark, populated it with fifty women and three men and sailed to Ireland. Another legend suggest that the stone pillow that Jacob slept on when he had his dream of angles ascending and descending from heaven became the Stone of Destiny on which Irish High Kings were crowned before it was given to the Scots. Jeremiah is thought to have visited Ireland and helped establish Brehon law on the principles of the Ten Commandments. The tradition of crowning a goat at the Puck Fair in Killorglin, Co Kerry is taken from the scapegoat of Leviticus chapter 16 and so on. While there is a fanciful element to all these traditions, at the start of the twentieth century a small group of British Israelites spent millions in today's terms digging at Tara convinced there were going to find the Ark of the Covenant. All this is tenuous. What would have changed the history of Ireland and indeed the world was a proposal by Robert Harrington to Oliver Cromwell that by making Ireland a homeland for the Jews Cromwell could solve his perceived Irish Catholic and European Jewish problems. Cromwell had a surprising enlightened policy towards Jews, given his view of Catholics, but he failed to support this ambitious scheme.

The first documented visit by Jews to Ireland is recorded in 1079 in the *Annals of Innisfallen* when five Jews came 'across the sea', probably from France, but left after a less than fulsome welcome. Small populations of Jews came to Ireland in the Middle Ages but the main influx came at the end of the nineteenth century. In 1882 the Russian Czar Alexander III introduced his infamous May Laws that made Jewish community life virtually impossible. Many migrated to Western Europe, including England and a number came to Ireland. Ireland was probably not the desired destination for many of these new
30

arrivals.   Unscrupulous ship captains docked in Cork and declared that they had arrived in New York.   Given the lack of English by most of these migrants, shouting 'New York' in Cork harbour, and being replied by 'Cork, Cork' from locals made the mistake understandable.   Whatever the reason, a small Jewish community became established in a number of Irish cities.

The experience of Jews in Ireland has generally been very positive.   Members of this community made rapid economic progress and within a generation were starting to make a distinct contribution to Irish society.   Over the last hundred years Jews have significantly contributed in areas such as business, medicine, academia, law, politics and the arts.   Dublin and Cork have had Jewish mayors and Fianna Fail, Fianna Gael and Labour have all had Jewish TDs.   Jews have represented Ireland at numerous sports and gone from here to contribute across the world including Chaim Herzog, the Irish born President of Israel.

Ireland's major anti-Semitic incident was the Limerick Pogrom of 1904-06.   A Redemptorist priest, Fr John Creagh, influenced a section of the Limerick population to undertake an economic blockade of the city's small Jewish population, many of whom were employed as small traders.   Over a two year period most of the Jewish population left Limerick.   The motivation for Creagh's action could be found in a perceived economic threat from the small incoming community or as a form of 'revenge' for the expulsion of Redemptorists from France, supposedly under Jewish influence.   During the Second World War neutral Ireland accepted only about sixty Jewish refugees and had in Charles Bewley a strongly anti-Semitic ambassador in Berlin.   While only one Irish born Jew died in the holocaust many Jews who had Irish relatives perished when they could and should have been allowed admittance to Ireland.   De Valera's visit to the German ambassador in Dublin to commiserate on the death of Hitler remains one of the stains on his legacy.   Yet this said, Ireland's Jews have normally seen Ireland as a country of refuge and a recently established Holocaust Memorial Day is a further sign of the importance the present Irish state gives to its Jewish citizens.

The Irish Jewish population peaked in the early 1960s at almost 10,000 but has declined over the past 50 years to barely 2,000. Dublin's Jewish museum bears eloquent testimony to the contribution of Jews to Ireland and today the Chief Rabbi is a regular participant at state occasions.

There is a similar positive story of acceptance and inclusion for Muslims in Ireland. There were historic interactions through the Viking capture of Irish and selling them on as slaves in the Middle East. Thomas Davis' ballad, *The Siege of Baltimore,* records a raid on the town by Muslim pirates in the seventeenth century but Ireland's history with Muslims has generally been far more positive than these incidents imply. Dean Mahomet came to Ireland in the late eighteenth century, married a local, published an account of his life and eventually moved to Brighton where he established a prosperous bath-house, the first in a succession of prosperous, cultured and successful Muslim residents in Ireland.

The first significant Muslim community to become established in Ireland comprised medical students who studied at the Royal College of Surgeons in Dublin, a number of whom remained in Ireland. One of these, Dr Moosajee Bhamjee, became Ireland's first Muslim TD in 1992. Economic links to the Muslim world have included Mivan Construction from Northern Ireland whose extensive contracts in the Middle East have included the renewal of the golden roof of Islam's third holist site, the Dome of the Rock mosque in Jerusalem. The Celtic Tiger, allied to the peace process in Northern Ireland, has witnessed significant Muslim migration into Ireland. Most cities now have at least one mosque and the Islamic Cultural Centre at Clonskeagh, south Dublin, is among the most significant religious buildings of twentieth century Ireland. In the wake of the attacks on New York and Washington on 11 September 2001, when there was a backlash against Muslim populations in many European cities, the Muslim experience in Ireland was very positive. The establishment of Muslim national schools, the translation of the Qur'an into Irish and development of a community structure all point to Muslims seeking to settle in Ireland. Ireland is the destination rather than a stage of a further migration. By 2005 there were approximately 30,000 Muslims settled in Ireland, more Muslims than Anglicans worship each weekend in Dublin and the largest faith based student society in University College Dublin is the Islamic Society.

There has been a similar proportional increase in the number of Hindus, Sikhs and Buddhists, even if their overall numbers are considerably smaller than Muslims. Ireland has other relig-ious communities such as Bahá'is and a plural Ireland is now a reality. The landscape is starting to be populated with temples, minarets and the other symbols of a multi-faith society.

So, what does this mean? Ireland is post-Christian because Christianity, including the varieties contained within it, is no longer the only religious option in Ireland. In state and society religion is no longer simply equated with one or two forms of Christianity. State ceremonies that have a religious involvement now have an increasingly diverse collection of clerics involved. Schools are starting to teach world religions as a course that includes Christianity as one religion among many and these same schools are rising to the challenge of a multi-faith population. Ecumenical organisations have been joined by inter-faith groups such as the Northern Ireland Inter-Faith Forum, the Dublin Three Faiths Forum and Christian-Jewish groups. While the religious landscape has become more complicated it has also become more interesting. The content-ion that religion in Ireland means Christianity is no longer valid. It is an exciting new world.

Post-Violence

Part of Ireland's charm is that its people normally only fight each other. The Irish do not go off invading other countries, at least not in the last 1500 years. However, a violent response to those who come here is a different story. Ever since the English interest in Ireland there has been conflict. The story of most of the second millennium is one of invasion, warfare, plantation, internal strife and a seemingly insurmountable problem.

This appears to have changed. After 1922 what became the Republic of Ireland slowly established itself as a viable European nation. Neutrality kept Ireland out of the Second World War and while violence around the border in the late 1950s, and particularly in the aftermath of Bloody Sunday in Derry in 1972, threatened this neutrality it did not involve the new state. The peace process in Northern Ireland since the early 1990s has brought spectacular changes, even if most were grudgingly conceded. The destruction of IRA weapons, the final withdrawal of British soldiers to barracks in 2007 and the establishment of a fully neutral police service all mark this transition.

Political violence is largely absent from today's Ireland, for the first time in a millennium, and it appears that the reasons for such violence are receding. Yet Ireland is hardly violence free. In Northern Ireland former paramilitaries still seek to control areas for criminal purposes while organised crime in the Republic of Ireland is endemic in a number of areas. An Ireland free of violence might be an unrealistic utopia but that such a possibility can at least be considered is a remarkable improvement. The enmity and bitterness that generations of Irish have endured and perpetuated has not gone but a different Ireland can be envisaged. The implications of this will be considered later. Suffice to say here that a post-violence Ireland brings new possibilities.

Post-Poverty

Ireland has never been a wealthy country, at least not until recently. There are relatively few natural resources and while it is a superb environment for growing grass, having just the right amount of sun, heat and rain, grass is not currently a path to untold riches. While a wide variety of crops can be grown, most find Ireland less than an ideal environment. Generations of English colonial rule ensured that the Irish economy had little chance to develop and neo-colonialism in the 1950s almost brought the struggling Republic of Ireland to its knees. The more industrial Northern Irish economy declined in the 1970s and 1980s as the traditional heavy industries of shipbuilding and aircraft manufacturing shed employees and struggled for survival. Car manufacturing, DeLorean style, was a short-lived fiasco. Under most economic indicators Northern Ireland was the poor cousin of the United Kingdom and the Republic of Ireland the poor man of Western Europe.

All this has changed. The 'peace dividend' of recent years in Northern Ireland has significantly boosted the economy with the EU and USA investing in infrastructure and regeneration projects. But the really dramatic change has come in the Republic of Ireland. Long-term EU investment, the development of a supportive tax regime and the utilisation of Ireland's main natural resource – a well educated, English speaking workforce – has transformed the nation into one of the highest per capita incomes in the world. Infrastructure now includes a developing motorway system, the Luas, the Port Tunnel and ambitious future plans. Ryanair, among others, shows a vibrant business sector not content to work just in Ireland but increasingly confident to participate as major economic players on the European and wider stage. The over inflation of house prices, to a degree fuelled by the return of part of the Irish Diaspora, has introduced a measure of relative poverty with the inability of many to get on the property ladder. There is still a small residue of rural poverty, there is far too much urban poverty and a new class of poor has arrived in Ireland. Asylum seekers are forming a bottom rung in society with some of the newly arrived economic migrants taking low paid jobs that the Irish no longer wish to have. Poverty has not completely disappeared, nor will it, but the change in the overall wealth of Ireland is remarkable and has created a new Ireland.

Post-Emigration

Whether it was 6th century monks in faith hoisting their sail to the wind or huddled masses forlornly taking their last gaze at their famine ravaged homeland, the Irish have always been travellers. In 1607 Hugh O'Neill, Earl of Tyrone, and Rory O'Donnell, Earl of Tyrconnell, along with almost one hundred of their retinue, sailed from Ireland to an uncertain future. The plantation of Ulster was followed by a further westward movement of what became known as the Scots Irish and mass migration from Ireland became the norm.

The years associated with the potato famine in the 1840s dramatically increased what had already become an established pattern. The difference was that while formerly the Irish had migrated for a better future, now they were leaving to try and just survive. As Irish people established themselves in the USA, Canada, Australia, and South Africa, migration to these new outposts of Ireland became increasingly attractive and the drain of population continued. Not all the Irish travelled that far. The Western British cities absorbed a significant proportion of the Irish population and London, Liverpool, Manchester, Birmingham and Glasgow all developed large Irish communities.

In the twentieth century migration showed no sign of abating. Economic difficulties, particularly in the 1930s, 1950s and 1980s, saw the Republic of Ireland unable to offer all its population a secure, employed future. The political violence on Northern Ireland resulted in a 'brain drain'. The standard route was for short-term third level education in Britain, but short-term too often became permanent.

This has changed. A combination of the peace process and Celtic Tiger has resulted in an Ireland needing to attract workers from across the world. The Dublin bus driver today might be Nigerian and the Belfast nurse from the Philippines. Dungannon is 20% Portuguese speaking and 25% of Gort's population is from Brazil. Immigration is an issue for the first time since the plantation of Ulster in the seventeenth century. Some Irish will still choose to leave, but today it is by choice rather than necessity. An Ireland that is now a destination rather than a point of embarkation creates many new missional opportunities.

Post-Independent
So far, the developing picture has been looking good to many. An improved, attractive Ireland is emerging. Yet has this new Ireland sold out on its independence? One reading of the peace process is a settlement and recognition of the reality of a British orientated community in Northern Ireland while another reading is the abandonment of the prospect of independence as an unattainable dream. The establishment of the Republic of Ireland was a foretaste of the independence most colonies attained from European powers after the Second World War. The struggles to survive financially through the 1950s were followed by the destabilisation of the Northern Irish conflict and then further economic difficulties.

Yet, as prosperity increased in the Republic of Ireland, the desire for dominion over Northern Ireland decreased to the extent that the constitutional claim to the province could be given up in support of peace. An Ireland that won independence from Britain became pro-Europe to the extent that aspects of independence have been surrendered to Brussels. Litres replaced gallons and kilometres replaced miles, even if miles per hour confusingly remained for a further generation. Ireland has embraced European legislation and at times has acted as a guinea pig for proposals, such as smoking bans, that were eventually introduced elsewhere. As Irish companies have recently expanded into Britain, Europe and beyond, British companies have taken an increasing stake in the Irish economy. Today's Irish High Street or shopping centre is virtually indistinguishable from its British counterpart.

Perhaps the most symbolic sign of post-independent Ireland was the change from the Punt to the Euro. Despite initial scepticism Ireland rapidly embraced the Euro, a sign of its European perspective. Was the loss of the Punt lamented? As one of Europe's shorter lived currencies it had a significant place in the establishment of independent Ireland. Yet economic progress meant that the Euro was a more practical alternative and allowed easier access to the rest of Europe. Britain is now surrounded by Euro economies but Irish independence from Britain has been changed to dependence on Europe.

Ireland may also have surrendered a measure of independence with regard to its foreign policy. While Ireland has remained neutral, allowing its troops to serve only with United Nations peace-keeping operations, the recent transit of American troops through Shannon on their way to Iraq and Afghanistan has challenged this independence. It became apparent that American troops, with their weapons, were travelling through Shannon in large numbers and so Ireland was supporting the American war effort. Even more problematic was the possibility that the USA had used Shannon for 'rendition', the illegal transfer of suspects to areas where torture could be used in interrogation. Given Ireland's family ties to USA and the considerable American investment in Ireland, a dispute with the western neighbour was not in Ireland's interest. Independent

Ireland is dependent on the USA and independence may have been short lived. The 2008 vote to reject the revised European 'Constitution' may reflect a perception that independence is still worth keeping.

Post-Religious

Is Ireland post-religious? For generations sociologists have pointed to secularisation as the future for all western European nations, with Ireland a stubborn exception to the norm. Has Ireland finally given in and followed the rest? The decline in attendance for most Christian denominations is marked, yet the recent arrival of immigrants, many of them strongly Christian, has brought a new vitality to Irish Christianity. The Irish Methodist Church in 2005 arrested a long period of decline, largely due to the influx into its churches of non-nationals and today in a number of congregations Irish born worshippers are in the minority. The rapid rise in the number of people from a Muslim, Hindu, Buddhist and Sikh backgrounds further challenges the idea that Ireland has become secularised. The secularisation thesis itself, whereby religion becomes privatised and ceases to be an important factor in public society, has been challenged across Europe. The decline in Christendom influence is a reality, but faith continues to impact public life. It has not withered and died as predicted, even in 'secular' Europe. Sharing this, Ireland is developing new patterns of spirituality and an understanding of this contemporary Irish spirituality forms the basis of the next chapter.

Questions
1   Is the new Ireland an improvement on the old?
2   What will Ireland look and feel like in 2030?
3   Compared to the past, is it easier or harder to be a Christian in today's Ireland?

Chapter Three:

Irish Spirituality

This book is about Christian mission. The first two chapters have pointed where Ireland has come from and roughly where it now finds itself. Religion and faith have changed but what has not happened is the much heralded secularisation. Ireland has not become secular. The decline of institutional Christianity does not equate to a decline in spirituality. Indeed, it can be argued that the opposite is true. The contemporary spiritual map of Ireland will now be drawn as a recognition of this as the context within which mission is to occur. Following an inaccurate map rarely helps a journey. A five year old map of Dublin is difficult to use today as major and more subtle changes have altered what on the surface may still look reasonably familiar.

It took the decline of Christendom for the plurality of Irish spiritualities to re-emerge. There is no longer a dominant or orthodox spirituality from which all others are deviations or dissensions. Christendom was monolithic by nature, alternatives were problematic and dealt with accordingly. 'Outside the Church there is no salvation' was coined to suppress Christian alternatives and any deviation was robustly dealt with. Today pluralism is the reality and so non-Christian spiritualities, or varieties within the Christian family, are not deviant or dangerous, they are simply different. Part of the implication of this is a lack of awareness in the general populace of the difference between some traditional Protestant denominations, Christian background cults and non-Christian religions. Various Christian spiritualities are by far the major spiritual expressions in Ireland. Alternatives are now, at worst, competitors in the field of religious varieties and Ireland is rapidly moving to a place where they complement each other in the spiritual patchwork of the nation.

Paganism alive and well

Irish spirituality is not just Christian; indeed much that is called Irish spirituality is far from Christian. Celtic spirituality, often seen as a form of Christian expression, has a life of its own and is clearly distinct from orthodox Christianity. When William Cleary was charged with burning his wife, Brigit, to death in 1895 in Co. Tipperary his defence was that fairies had taken his wife replacing her with a weak 'changeling' and an ordeal by fire was the only way to entice the fairies to return Brigit. While this understanding does not indicate a widespread Irish belief in such phenomena, it does illustrate that 1500 years of Christianity have not eradicated pre-Christian beliefs. Contemporary Irish spirituality is Christian, pagan, diverse, confused, eclectic and more beside. This is the environment in which mission now happens. This chapter asks 'What is contemporary Irish spirituality?' and considers the implications for mission.

Pilgrimage

The Irish have long been a pilgrim people and this appears to have remained, at least in part, as an element of the Irish psyche. Pilgrimage, as a Christian activity, may have been invented by Emperor Constantine's mother but the Irish were early participants. As early as the seventh century Irish kings are noted as participating in pilgrimage to Rome and Jerusalem, often through the record of their death on pilgrimage. Part of the spirituality of the Celtic saints was in their understanding of journey as pilgrimage. Reaching a destination was part of this, but the journey itself was a spiritual exercise and undertaken for its own sake. A modern equivalent is the pilgrimage trail to Santiago de Compostello in northern Spain that has recently witnessed a dramatic upsurge of popularity.

Lough Derg and Croagh Patrick are, year on year, witnessing an increase of pilgrims willing to undertake the arduous activities associated with these pilgrimages. Glendalough is another traditional pilgrimage site that is increasing in popularity but that may have more to do with its rebranding as a tourist destination within easy reach of south Dublin. So why are traditional Catholic pilgrimage sites increasing in popularity? Institutional Catholicism is in decline and many of the more penitential aspects of traditional Catholicism, such as confession, have all but disappeared. Increasing interest in pilgrimage is not a sign of a revival of traditional Catholicism. Rather it is an example of a postmodern interest in spirituality that is not being met in traditional forms of Irish Christianity. Croagh Patrick, in particular, connects to forms of pilgrimage going back perhaps 5000 years linking a developing form of Christian spirituality to its pre-Christian roots. The twenty-five thousand or more that visit Croagh Patrick on Reek Sunday each July may not rival the great Hindu Maha Kumbh Mela that can attract twenty-five million devotees every twelfth year but does show mass pilgrimage as a significant religious factor in postmodern Ireland.

In most contemporary pilgrimages the individual sets the agenda and the pace. There is no requirement for group uniformity, to do the same thing as a group of people in the same way at the same time with others. There may be a norm but it is open to personal interpretation. The individual is key and the religious experience takes whatever form the individual desires. There is no requirement to affirm dogma or theological formulations nor is there a personal morality that must confirm to religiously sanctioned criteria. Rather, the pilgrimage experience is whatever the participant wants it to be. It is the ultimate consumer driven form of religious participation. The traditional three-day Lough Derg pilgrimage of fasting, barefoot penance and lack of sleep has been supplemented, since 1992, by a one-day version that is more congenial to the contemporary mind and body; surely a fine example of moving with the times.

All this has helped to spawn a spirituality industry whereby what is called 'Irish Spirituality' or 'Celtic Spirituality' is marketed across the world and people come to experience something of the 'Irish Spirit'. A cynic might view this as a commercial exploitation of the postmodern desire for spiritual experience, the popularity of which has been increasing in recent years. This brings a challenge to Irish Christianity as there is certainly an opportunity for the Irish Church to use this interest in Celtic spirituality as a means of evangelisation. Yet the caution is that an increase of interest in spirituality is not an increase of interest in being part of an institutional religion or mainstream religious community. Spirituality is something that many perceive can be dipped into as much or as little as an individual wishes. It is a postmodern eclectic form of religious consumerism that wants individual spiritual products without having to accept a complete overall package. Can the Church use this interest in spirituality to point people to the living Christ? Or will the promotion of Celtic spirituality point people to this 'product' but away from an orthodox Christian faith?

Miracle and Magic

A different form of spirituality is found at Knock (and in the multitude of Irish accents that are heard at Lourdes, Fatima, Assisi and elsewhere). While Knock, like Croagh Patrick and Lough Derg, might appear to be a classic symbol of conservative Catholic belief, the reality is that it resonates with a different and older form of Irish spirituality. A belief in spirits, fairies, leprechauns, 'the little people' and so on is not far from the surface in Ireland. While some of this can be explained as a primitive form of rural superstition, it is a little harder to use this explanation when asking a twenty-first century Irish farmer why he drives his €100,000 tractor around a thorn thicket in the middle of a single field that is worth several million euro. This fairy thorn still remains, perhaps not a defined belief but as an unexplained phenomenon that it is better (or at least easier) not to challenge. Modernity, to some extent, bypassed an Ireland that was transformed from a pre-industrial rural economy into a postmodern society that is content to allow the unexplained to stay just that. Modernity wanted everything to be scientifically explained. Postmodernity allows mystery to remain and Ireland is happy to oblige.

Miracles are believed and accepted today, in a way surprising to a previous generation, and so the faithful at Knock may be influenced as much by postmodernity as by Christian devotion. Is the popularity of Knock a help to mission in Ireland? Possibly not. Many visiting Knock are there because of an interest in spirituality and openness to the mystery of life. There may be a cure for serious illness found at Knock (or Lourdes and Fatima), but that might be explained as much in terms of magic as in faith. The desire to fast track the beatification of the late Pope John Paul II, and the subsequent need for a verifiable miracle, buys into this mood. The scientific evidence to verify such a miracle, so important in modernity, is no longer seen as essential. A vaguer acceptance that something that cannot be explained has occurred is enough. But the vagueness of this explanation points to a weakened link between a miracle and Christian faith. Magic is replacing miracle with faith the casualty.

It might be that some sort of Irish 'folk religion' deserves a place here. Traditional beliefs that owe at least something to Celtic roots still survive. The influence of such beliefs as a controlling factor in lives is hard to determine. Folk lore, tradition and superstition are all prevalent in an older generation but not so much in those David McWilliams christened 'the Pope's Children', the recipients of Ireland's recent economic success.

New Age

Despite the designation 'New Age' now sounding quite old fashioned, this diverse form of spirituality has been centred in Ireland for almost thirty years. In the 1980s southern and western Ireland were among the most underdeveloped areas of Western Europe. For those looking for a rural idyll in order to escape from the economic and cultural pressures of fast-paced, money driven, urban European life, West Cork and in particular Cool Mountain became the must have address. On the hillside a distinct community developed that eschewed modernity in favour of a simpler and more basic lifestyle. Tepees and caravans proliferated, without the benefit of electricity, mains water or most other 'essentials' of life, and a several hundred strong community developed. Part of a wider 'New Age Traveller culture' of the 1980s, this diverse community shared certain spiritual values and lifestyle choices, and attracted people though this spirituality and way of life. Cool Mountain has declined in popularity in recent years although a small alternative community still exists there. Although never as well developed as the alternative community of Nimbin, Australia, Cool Mountain is still an important representative of the diverse makeup of contemporary Irish spirituality.

Hinduism and Buddhism

For the last number of years, normally sometime in autumn, Sri Mata Amritanandamyi Devi visits Ireland and conducts 'hugging seminars'. These are roughly what you might expect – teaching on and the experience of hugging. Known as 'the hugging saint', Amma exhibits one form of Hindu spirituality that, while not affecting Ireland as a whole, does have an impact on at least a small part of the population for a period. This form of spirituality is relatively mainstream, albeit a tad unusual for Ireland.

There are over thirty Buddhist retreat centres in Ireland ranging from a room above shops to a country estate. Given this number, it could be argued that Buddhism, after Christianity, is the most significant spiritual influence on contemporary Ireland. These centres represent many different expressions of Buddhism and operate chiefly as places of meditation. Some run weekly courses; others are able to offer weekend retreat programmes. Many who utilise these centres use them as a form of spiritual health farm – a place to come to detoxify mind, body and spirit and basically chill out in a contemplative atmosphere. Indeed many mainstream health spas offer therapies that owe much to Buddhism arguably increasing further a Buddhist influence on Ireland.

Part of the attraction of these spiritualities is their lack of a metanarrative or the need to provide an answer to every aspect of life. In a postmodern society there is a suspicion of religions, such as Christianity, that present an overarching answer and offer a complete spiritual package. Christianity does not want to impact an area of an individual's life, it needs to convert, save and transform the whole person and community. A number of the forms of Hindu and Buddhist spirituality presently developing in Ireland do not have this impetus. They are able to be an almost leisure activity for the religiously curious and so avoid the 'take it all or leave it' impression that Christianity gives.

Riverdance and all that

If Cool Mountain has declined in significance, a newer and very vibrant form of Irish spiritual expression is found in the marketing phenomenon that is Riverdance and its associated varieties. Within this could be included such diverse entities as Ryanair, the Celtic Tiger, Croke Park, Irish racehorses and even the national soccer and rugby teams. They are all examples of success, something Ireland is not particularly used to. Survival, north and south, has normally been achievement enough but the advent of Ireland as a vibrant, successful and peaceful island has introduced the 'success' word to the Irish vocabulary. Irish now lead the world in some of the areas listed above and a spirituality of success is becoming part of the Irish psyche. This success is breeding a generation whose main religion might well be a form of hedonism, living primarily for the moment and seeking pleasure, entertainment and the gratification of desire. The delayed gratification that used to be such a prominent characteristic of a rural life that looked to growing cycles and generations has been replaced by a population who think about today rather than tomorrow. The hedonistic lifestyle of many in Ireland will have a consequence in the (near) future greater than is already apparent.

It is not just an economic success. It is more than certain industries or aspects of Irishness doing extremely well. These Irish success stories appear to add something to Ireland and its people. They are becoming part of the Irish personality in the way that priests, Guinness and emigration were earlier hallmarks. This spirituality of success is not equated to the Calvinist work ethic that was so influential in Northern Ireland in previous generations. The success of Irish enterprise is not put down to hard work. Rather imagination, innovation, risk taking and 'the luck of the Irish' are seen as contributing factors. Instead of exporting devout but impoverished Christians throughout the world, Ireland now exports successful entrepreneurs and entertainers whose achievement is linked with their Irishness. Economic success is not equated with Christian faith nor viewed in opposition to faith. Faith has simply been privatised and become one component of a total spiritual identity that is marked by success as well as other factors. Rather than God deciding latterly to bless the Irish, the Irish perceive themselves as sorting out their nation themselves. The Protestant work ethic has been fully secularised and the reinvented into a new form of spirituality that helps define what it means to be Irish.

The Spirit of the Age

G K Chesterton argued that when people stopped believing in God, rather than believing in nothing they would believe in anything. This has perhaps never been better illustrated than in the western world in the early twenty-first century. The spirit of the age is to believe in anything and Ireland is no exception to this. The success of Dan Brown's *The Da Vinci Code*, and the plethora of writing in this genre, illustrates this. On television the 'X Files', 'Charmed', 'Buffy', 'Primeval', even the resurgence of 'Dr Who', all point to this interest in the unexplained. Part of the attraction of this area is that the unexplained remains just that. The only unifying feature is that the final pages of the book or last minute of the film/TV programme do not have a neat ending that explains everything in rational terms. Mystery remains mystery and while certain answers may be pointed to, there is no comprehensive explanation. The truth remains 'out there' but many different possibilities exist. Objective truth is downplayed and Christianity, based on prepositional truth, faces a challenge.

In June 1998 the Irish UFO Society was founded. This is not a major organisation but it has held two international UFO conferences in Ireland and is building up accounts of sightings that it reports 'do, of course, remain confidential'. Ireland does not appear to be a hotbed of UFO activity, but there is a small but growing group of people interested in such phenomena and seeking reports of sightings, abductions and other associated activity. The Irish, as much as anyone else, are captive to the contemporary willingness to believe in almost anything.

Humanism

Part of a wider movement opposed to traditional religion and promoting free thinking – in many ways a direct response to Ireland's Christendoms – a Humanist group was founded in Dublin in 1967. It met for around ten years and involved such notables as Justin Keating - a TD and government minister, and Owen Sheehy Skeffington. The group eventually folded as its members became involved in other related issues; Dr Jim Loughran became the first chair of the Irish Family Planning

Association and Bill and Aine Hyland influential in the multi-denominational school movement.

The Humanist Association of Ireland was formed in 1993 under the leadership of Dick Spicer, a founder member of the Campaign to Separate Church and State in the 1980s. Members hold ceremonies to name babies, for marriage and death and in 1997 *The Humanist Philosophy: With an Irish Guide to Non-Religious Ceremonies* was published. Major celebrations are Darwin Day on 10 February and World Humanist Day on 21 June. A Northern Ireland group exists and a local group was recently established in Sligo.

The Humanist Association of Ireland and the Ulster Humanists are part of a major international movement but have had little impact in Ireland. While many people may share some aspects of their philosophy, few appear to want to associate with them. In some ways the groups exist as a contradiction. Opposed to the role of organised Christianity in Ireland, the Irish Humanists do not seem to have a similar critique of other organised religions found here. The Christendom heritage of Ireland makes this historically appropriate but the developing multi-faith context will show whether the groups are truly humanist or simply anti-Christian.

Have Irish Humanists developed their own loose religious understanding? They do not have clergy or a creed but neither do others such as Quakers. Part of the Humanist contradiction is their very existence as a form of institutional religion, even if loosely defined. The Humanist rites of passage relating to birth, marriage and death underpin a particular spiritual understanding of life. As such they are a small but distinct contribution to the contemporary spiritual map of Ireland.

New Forms of Christianity

Christianity has provided much of the spirituality that has been and still is found in Ireland. There have been many forms of Christian spirituality experienced in Ireland of which the umbrella term of 'Celtic spirituality' only encompasses a segment. Ireland has normally been part of the Christian mainstream and various expressions of Christian spirituality, from Benedictine chanting to the not dissimilar Scots Presbyterian singing the Psalms without music, have all helped to give voice to Christian faith in Ireland. Today there are a number of new forms of Christian spirituality developing in Ireland.

Charismatic Christianity: While not quite at the forefront of Pentecostal Christianity, Ireland, or more precisely Monaghan, was the birthplace of a major Pentecostal denomination. In 1915, just nine years after what is generally considered the birth of the modern Pentecostal movement in Los Angeles, the Welsh evangelist George Jeffreys founded the Elim Pentecostal Church in Monaghan which has gown to over 9,000 congregations spread across approximately forty countries. Pentecostal congregations have been a feature of most towns in Northern Ireland since then but it is in the last decade that Pentecostal Christianity has become more widespread. The strength of the traditional protestant denominations in Northern Ireland had hidden the growth of Pentecostal Christianity from many although during 'The Troubles' one of the many horrific incidents involved a small independent Pentecostal congregation. In 1983 three worshippers were murdered and seven others injured in an attack on Mountain Lodge Pentecostal Church near Darkley, Co. Armagh. The church was also burned in 1995.

Charismatic Christianity differs from Pentecostal Christianity only in a denominational sense. Both movements share the same basic beliefs and expressions of faith but charismatic Christians are found in what are described as the mainstream denominations, the Roman Catholic, Anglican, Methodist and Presbyterian Churches. The Charismatic movement developed in the early 1960s and spread to Ireland within a couple of years. Thousands of individuals and dozens of parishes were initially impacted in a development that affected both Catholic and Protestant congregations. Clergy and lay, Protestant and Catholic, sharing together in Charismatic prayer meetings were among the original features but more recently the movement has developed in a couple of ways. There are fewer dramatic events and major gatherings and the ecumenical dimension has declined but this decline has been offset by a gradually increasing interest in this expression of Christianity, particularly

48

in Protestant denominations. To some extent, what seemed radical in the 1960s has become more commonplace today.

African Christianity: Nigeria is of particular interest to Irish Christians as it was one of the very few countries that had significant numbers of both Irish Catholic and Protestant missionaries. Irish Catholic missionaries had gone first to their Diaspora, then often to areas of French influence as early Catholic missionaries were often trained by French orders and then to other areas of general Catholic influence. Protestant missionaries, while also going to their Diaspora, went largely to areas of British influence and so despite very large missionary movements there was relatively little interaction between Irish Catholic and Protestant missionaries abroad.

Nigeria was a significant exception to this. Bishop Shanahan of Co Tipperary was a foundational figure in Nigerian Catholicism serving there from 1902-1932. A contemporary was Revd Paul Kingston from Co Cork who was a pivotal figure in Nigerian Methodism and in the translation of Scripture. By the 1960s there were dozens of Irish Protestant and around two thousand Catholic missionaries in Nigeria, a number of whom came to prominence in the Biafran war. True to their vocation these missionaries remained with their congregations, schools and hospitals and served all in need regardless of political outlook. Irish people listened intently to news of the conflict and how it affected their fellow nationals. Money raised for the 'black babies' was a normal part of Irish Catholicism but no-one foresaw the subsequent development. In the late 1990s the Celtic Tiger needed workers and Nigeria provided many who had a prior contact with Ireland through the missionaries. These Nigerians have brought various expressions of faith with them and a number of Anglican, Methodist and Catholic parishes have noted a significant increase in membership. Many of the Nigerian migrants are members of indigenous denominations and a number of these have set up congregations in various Irish towns. They have become a distinct feature of Irish Christianity and, rather than an exotic accessory, are becoming part of the mainstream such as the Church of the Cherubim and Seraphim that has been a member of the Irish Council of Churches for a number of years.

Nigerians, and Christians from a wide variety of African countries, are rapidly becoming Irish citizens and contributing to what it means to be Irish. This is as much in the realm of Irish Christianity and spirituality as in other fields. There is no one expression of African Christianity. Some come with an exuberant form of Pentecostal expression, some have a very traditional understanding more akin to Irish Protestantism and Catholicism in the 1950s, some have a form of Christianity that appears to owe much to elements of African Traditional Religion. The African Christianities that are increasingly found in Ireland are adding far more than one dimension to the spirituality of Ireland.

Eastern European Christianity: Catholicism has benefited significantly from the arrival of thousands of eastern Europeans. Many parishes now have masses in Polish among other languages and priests are coming to support their faith communities. Instead of Irish priests following their congregations to Boston, Polish priests are following their people to Dublin. There are a smaller number of Eastern European Protestant Christians, most of which have become integrated into existing congregations although there are a small number of language-based congregations in Dublin.

Yet the story is more complex than this. For example, in Dungannon a Brazilian missionary works among residents originally from places as diverse as Mozambique and East Timor but who share the Portuguese language. Ireland never had only one form of Christian spirituality. It has always been in the plural; the difference today is simply the number of variations. Whilst commonplace in Europe and North America, such diversity is only now becoming apparent in Ireland.

Spiritual Direction: Since the decline of the Druids, Irish people have normally gone to Christian clergy for spiritual direction. Indeed, at different times these figures have also given a great deal of political, economic and social direction. In recent years a largely lay movement has developed offering a form of Christian spiritual direction. The All Ireland Spiritual Guidance Association was formed in 2002 as an umbrella group for practitioners who accompany individuals on their spiritual journey as a 'soul friend'. The practice shares much in common with forms of psychological therapy and follows a normally monthly regular meeting. The sessions are confidential, the spiritual directors generally are members of the recognised body and often equipped with a MA from Milltown Institute and they receive payment from those they support. In a session a Spiritual Director seeks to listen in an empathetic and contemplative manner, discerning the move of the Spirit in a person's life to bring healing and wholeness from past hurts. The desired result is an individual who experiences spiritual growth, healing and transformation. Just how close this conforms to orthodox Christianity varies depending on the Director. It is certainly a challenge to the role of Christian clergy in providing guidance and direction. The growth of this movement coinciding with the decline in the importance of clergy is a pointer than secularisation is not significantly happening. The reality is that the needs of people that were formerly met by orthodox Christianity are now being met in an increasingly diverse number of ways.

Conferences and Retreat Houses: In recent years retreat houses and conference centres, often run by Catholic orders or evangelical para-church groups, have become increasingly popular. Parish groups will book themselves in for a weekend that is often part spiritual retreat and part holiday. There is often a speaker, seminar programme and the fellowship of living, eating and playing together. Castlewellan Castle, set in Castlewellan Forest Park, Co Down, is an example of a centre run by an evangelical para-church group. Congregations will book into the centre, bring their own speaker and programme and use the conducive atmosphere of the centre for their retreat. On other occasions the castle management themselves put on programmes that people attend as individuals. For the last twenty years the Methodist Church has run a holiday week each August based in the castle and its grounds attended by about 700 people. Other large events include Summer Madness, a camp run by an ecumenical, through largely Anglican, group at the start of each July attended by around 5000 young people. A similar number attend 'New Horizons' Bible week each summer in Coleraine and there are many smaller versions.

Typical of the many Catholic retreat houses are Grace Dieu Manor, Waterford run by the Missionaries of the Sacred Heart and Drumalis, Larne with the Sisters of the Cross and Passion. In both houses there are facilities for groups to be hosted and opportunities for individuals to come and share in programmes run by the resident staff. In comfortable surroundings individuals might participate in a programme aimed at those searching for a vocation, support groups for those recently bereaved or divorced, investigate Christian perspectives on ecological issues or take part in arts based events.

These expressions of Christianity exhibit a depth of commitment by Christians who want to spend a significant part of their holidays in spiritual retreat and 'fun' Christian activities. It may example dissatisfaction with the local church community the individual is part of, the implication that such participation does not provide all the spiritual nourishment that the individual needs. There is a negative aspect in that it can reflect a desire to withdraw from engagement with the wider world and retreat into a 'holy huddle'. In a society where Christianity is increasingly on the margins Christians can desire to live, at least for a week, in a temporary form of Christendom where everything is based on Christian faith, people think and act in a way that is expected and the world is 'as it should be'. Yet perhaps this is at the heart of what retreat means – going to a place and time when a relationship with Christ can be refreshed in a supportive atmosphere so that the rest of the year can be faced with renewed energy and hope.

U2 Christianity: Is there such a thing as U2 Christianity? If not, there is something very close. Theologians write about the spiritual journey of U2, the gospel as understood in their lyrics and in the last few years a trend has developed for a small number of congregations to hold U2charist services. In such services the church resembles a nightclub or concert venue, the 'hymns' are U2 songs and the liturgy is based around the spiritual themes flowing from the lyrics. Often the service will take a 'world justice' theme to tie in with some of Bono's social and ethical causes. Such events have an evangelistic intent in that, when widely advertised, the hope is to attract a generation who are 'into' U2 but not institutional Christianity. At a second level it exhibits an honest attempt to overcome the sacred/ secular divide that has captured much of Christianity and express faith in a culturally relevant form. What it is not is an attempt to create the Church of U2 with Bono as a type of Christ-like Saviour.

Once more this form of spirituality, as in most of the developing forms of Irish Christian spirituality, reflects dis- satisfaction with institutional Christianity. More positively, that it can be embraced by mainstream Christianity offers hope that a missional engagement is possible with a culture that will attend U2 concerts in vast numbers but shows less desire to participate in regular Christian activities.

Wicca

Where does Wicca come into the picture? During the middle years of the last century Irish Catholic clergy were quick to label 'pagan' many aspects of modernity they opposed, but that understanding of paganism does not equate with Wicca as a distinct spiritual understanding. Neither does a simple delve into Ireland's past equate Celtic religion, perhaps with a touch of New Age, as Wicca.

Possibly the best example of Wicca as a living contemporary spirituality in Ireland is found in the Anam Holistic Healing Centre near Blessington, Co Wicklow. Operating in a similar way to Buddhist meditation centres or some of the Christian retreat and conference centres, Anam offers individuals and small group seminars and workshops in subjects such as shamanism, dowsing, tantra yoga and individual spiritual direction. The roots of this form of spirituality certainly go back into Ireland's Celtic past but Wicca is far from Druidism reborn. It is linked to similar movements across the world that draw resources from various expressions of primal religion and seeks to create a spirituality rooted in the past that works in a contemporary developed world context. Wicca in Ireland is linked with other movements, considered by some to be more neutral, for example, the Irish Society of Diviners, founded in 1958. There are other cross- overs to psychics, mediums, fortune tellers and other forms of spiritualism.

Is this devil worship? Well, it is not easy to say. Wicca will portray itself as a distinct spirituality in Ireland and does need to be recognised as part of the spiritual makeup of the land. Whether it is helpful or harmful is a different question that is not easy to answer. Certain expressions of Christianity have been proven to be very damaging in Ireland so this is a much wider issue. Wicca certainly calls on spirits that are far from Christian but so do many other spiritual understandings. To put a Christian perspective on Wicca and seek to condemn it would require the same spotlight and questions on all other spiritualities in Ireland, and also for Christianity to be equally judged under the same criteria. That said, it is still possible to argue that Wicca does invoke spiritual powers that many Christians understand as demonic. That is an objective assessment and not pejorative. There are many spiritual understandings that have harmed people in Ireland. Wicca may be a public face of one such movement, but on almost any criteria it is not unique.

Missional Implications

Irish spirituality is now a complex and varied item. Christianity has become one form of spirituality among many and there are a number of missionary spirits at work of which Christianity is one but only one among others.

In the spiritual makeup of Ireland, to some extent Christianity is conceived as being of the past and to have 'failed'. A perception may be that Christianity has had its chance and now there are new alternatives. This negative image puts Christianity at a disadvantage. Whatever the reality, this is the perception of at least some.

When Irish people think of spirituality today many do not think of Christianity. It is considered a religion whereas other faiths are viewed as spiritualities. In the average large Irish bookshop there is a small section for Christianity and a far larger section dealing with 'mind, body and spirit'. For the last couple of generations Christians considered the Church to be a spiritual entity in an increasingly secular world. While they were thinking that, the reality was that the Church was becoming a secular

54

body in an increasingly spiritual world. Consequently spiritual seekers, of which there are a growing number, find little reason to include institutional Christianity in their search, although non traditional forms of Christianity are a little more attractive. Indeed, the further from mainstream Christianity the better the attraction to many.

There are missional opportunities available to the Church to re-engage with this spiritual world. At the 'mind, body, spirit' fairs there are a host of spiritual seekers and a multitude of spiritual products on offer, but little that relates to mainstream Christianity. The Church needs to understand that in an Ireland of many spiritual possibilities the Church needs to go to people rather than passively expecting people to turn to the Church. This necessary reorientation for the Church allows it to understand itself more in terms of one movement among many others. The Church is forced to reinvent itself in terms of spirituality rather than as an institution. The dominant, arrogant Christendom perspectives are lost and a humble, deliberately attractive and intentionally spiritual movement can emerge. What is forced on Christianity by the changed religious climate of Ireland could prove to be one the features that transforms Irish Christianity from an institution into a movement. Whether this is happening or not is considered in the next chapter.

Questions

1   What is your experience of Christianity as just one religious option among many in contemporary Ireland?

2   Has your local church become marginalized in your community?

3   What does it mean to be Irish today?

Chapter Four:

The Accidental Rebirth of a Movement

Groucho Marx famously stated that he would never join an institution that was willing to have him as a member. The best man's speech joke is that marriage is a wonderful institution, but 'who wants to be in an institution?'. Despite the lack of attraction of an institution – Christianity has been an institution for much of its time in Ireland. A common definition is to consider an institution as a structure or mechanism of social order to govern and control the behaviour of a group of people. This is neither positive nor negative, but simply the way it is.

Institutions, particularly in a postmodern society, are increasingly unpopular with a growing dislike for control, rules and regulations. Individual choice and freedom is valued over societal conformity and so an institution is contrasted with a movement that can be defined as 'a change in position' or 'the activities of a group of people to achieve a specific goal'. There is a fluidity and spontaneity in a movement that is lacking in the institution. Consequently, even if they were almost perfect, the Christian institution and its various individual institutions are problematic in the twenty-first century just for being institutional.

In a postmodern society any organised structure, be it a political party, community group or Church, suffers because the mood of the time is not to want to commit to such groups that are structured hierarchically, are detailed and require a significant input of time. Institutions in Ireland are declining and the Church is not bucking this trend. Yet this institutional decline allows the possibility for Christianity to be reborn as a movement. That the various denominations do not desire this is irrelevant. The argument of this chapter is that certain aspects of the decline of Christianity as an institution are allowing Christianity as a movement to develop spontaneously.

The South African missiologist David Bosch argued for paradigm shifts in mission thinking as essential to understand reality. This book calls for an Irish Christian paradigm shift. Christianity has been conceived in institutional terms for most of its 1500 years in Ireland. The Synod of Whitby in 664, with the victory of Roman Christianity over Celtic Christianity, was also the victory of Christianity as an institution and this was maintained for the next 1300 years. It may be that it is the twenty first century that sees the necessary rebirth of Christianity as a movement. This may be happening in an unrecognised way already. The recognition, development and implementation of this may be the Irish paradigm shift needed.

Societal changes

Ireland has not usually been more progressive than much of the world but contemporary Ireland, especially the Republic of Ireland, finds itself among Europe's more postmodern nations. It is hard to define just what postmodernity is. The designation itself admits to what it is not. Modernity, stemming from the Enlightenment and scientific advancement, sought to provide explanations and solutions to all of humanity's problems. Just when this broke down is hard to determine. The World War One battlefields, where the industrial nations of Europe destroyed each other through technology, is one claimant. A similar claim is made for the Holocaust when science and technology were harnessed to exterminate almost half the Jewish race. Perhaps it was the 1960s when the teenager was born, societal cohesion started to collapse and the taboos of many generations were overcome in a decade. What is clear is that today society does not have confidence in science to answer its problems. Indeed, global warming is but one example where the destruction of humanity could be caused by technology rather than averted as modernity thought.

Postmodernity has no defining characteristics and to attempt definition is not to understand the nature of postmodernity. But there are recognisable features that challenge the continuation of Christianity as an institution. Postmodernity does not have one overarching or all encompassing story to explain everything, nor does it desire such. What is true for one no longer is considered as necessarily having validity for another. Truth has become relative. The nature of an institution is that there is a way to understand that needs to be accepted by all. Within a movement, however, there is a more eclectic approach.

Modernity subsumed personal choice within the need for the overall 'machine' to work. People worked in organisations, knowing their place in the hierarchy and followed clearly defined predetermined roles. In postmodernity personal choice is valued, individualism is encouraged and personal initiative recognised – characteristics that fit into a fluid movement rather than a rigid institution.

Institutions like to define the areas of their influence yet the contemporary world is created by mass media. What has been handed down for generations can be overturned in a weekend. Our parents relied on recognised authorities, be they Church, politicians, educationalists or even nobility, for their understanding of reality. Today we 'Google' to find our understanding and interpret between alternative perspectives. My understanding will not be your understanding; it will be determined by interpretation at least as much as facts.

Science, law and business are considered to be in the realm of public truth whereas faith has been privatised. Therefore, even where faith can be shown to have a dramatic effect on an individual, clearly transforming a person for the better, because it is private truth it is not considered to have validity beyond the individual who has been impacted.

Traditionally, authority normally was ceded to people and institutions because of the position held. These authorities changed very gradually and the Church was one of the fixtures in society. Postmodernity has swept away most of these formerly fixed points, the Church included. The authority of an institution has been replaced by the relationships within a movement. Yet the Church still operates on a hierarchical authority structure. A reliance on this approach places the Church in the past rather than the present.

There is much that the Church can do about these issues, but there is a fact from which it cannot escape. The Church is old. In a society that has abandoned so much that is old and lasting in favour of what is temporary, the longevity of the Church points to it being an historic institution. Its very durability is a pointer to the past.

The demise and possible imminent death of institutional Christianity in Ireland need not be a problem for Christianity. It is certainly a huge problem for institutional Christianity but Christianity has always existed beyond the confines of the institution. It can be argued that Christianity only became institutionalised after the conversion of Constantine and this was a sign of the success of the movement called Christianity. When it did not have any political, cultural or economic advantages, Christianity did very well. People were converted, community needs were met and the faith advanced. The 'problem' of institutional Christianity was in part an issue caused by the success of the Christian movement.

Roman Catholicism

For centuries Irish Catholicism has been a male controlled and led organisation supported by the passive loyalty of women. The important ministry of women in Scripture is clear and a rediscovery of the role of the Abbess in early Irish Christianity further demonstrates the inclusive nature of early Christian leadership but male domination has been the norm for centuries. Male clergy have supplied the parish personnel needed for the Irish Church for much of the twentieth century and a surplus has been exported in great numbers. This has changed. The decline in vocations has not yet had its full impact on Ireland but the next twenty years will see this unfolding. Irish Catholicism is only starting to see the unravelling of its structure, such as daily communion being cancelled in many parishes due to a lack of clergy. This manpower (and it is manpower) difficulty can be solved in a number of ways to prop up the institution. The importation of foreign clergy, a reversal of how Irish clergy have been used in places such as Britain and USA, will be attempted and is relatively unproblematic. Poland has become the new Ireland with regard to a clerical surplus. More radical alternatives that are largely beyond the power of the Irish hierarchy include accepting married priests or even female priests. Both of these are unlikely short-term solutions but one or both is still very possible by the middle of this century.

Yet this increasing shortage of clergy is being tackled in ways that allow a movement to emerge out of the problem. The decline in clergy allows an increased role for lay people, even if that causes some theological and organisational difficulties. Should a parish collapse because there is no resident priest? The answer is obviously no and throughout Ireland lay people are increasingly undertaking responsibilities that were formerly in the control of priests. Responsibilities for the upkeep of buildings are being taken over but more importantly are the roles of teaching and communicating the faith in which lay people are increasingly becoming prominent. Some of these are in 'official' positions. In secondary schools and third level colleges the traditional role of the chaplain, with a strong liturgical and sacramental emphasis, is being developed to focus more on counselling and student support with lay Catholics increasingly filling these paid positions. Here the shortage of suitable clergy rather than a shortage of clergy is the driving force. In an area where younger clergy normally served there is a dearth of young clergy. If there is not yet a crisis due to a lack of clergy there is already a significant problem due to a clear shortage of younger clergy. This change to lay chaplaincy is a very positive solution that enables a movement rather than bolsters a clerical institution. The lay status also means that the sacramental side of the role in increasingly carried out in conjunction with a local parish and so the faith within the educational institution is of necessity linked to that of a parish rather than being isolated. Young Catholic students increasingly experience faith within a parish setting rather than divorced in an educational institution. A further advantage is that these lay Catholic employees generally have less attachment and loyalty to the institutional Church. This does not mean they have a jaundiced view of the institution but rather they have no need to defend the structures and official line of the Church. What is good will be supported; what is not will be ignored or opposed. Clergy, bound in to a loyalty to the institution, only rarely became critics, even when there were apparent institutional problems. Irish Christianity would have benefited greatly from a more critical attitude by clergy and some of the mistakes of the past may have been avoided, or at least ameliorated.

There is a further factor related to educational institutions that is enabling the rebirth of a movement. For generations the sacramental preparation of Catholic children occurred in the parish schools usually led by Catholic teachers. The close link between school and parish has been diminishing in recent years but of more significance has been the decline in faith of many teachers within the Catholic educational system and the employment of teachers who are not from a Catholic background. Teachers are no longer the obvious people to pass on the Catholic faith to pupils. This role needs to be taken up by parents and the local parish. The response of some parishes has been to have clergy go to the schools to prepare children for first communion. More often it has been committed lay Catholics, appointed by the local parish, who are doing the sacramental preparation. Faith is increasingly being taught and transmitted by lay people who are personally committed to their beliefs and have the desire to see others understand faith and experience God in communion. An institutional approach is dying out and a more fluid pragmatic response is being developed. Catholic children are learning about faith from those who are personally committed to this task rather than those, either teachers or clergy, who had been employed by institutions to carry out this function.

During the 1970s some lay people discovered a measure of equality with priests and nuns during the era of charismatic renewal. In these groups lay and ordained had similar experiences, approached scripture in a fresh way without reading it through a Church conditioned interpretation, often met ecumenically and something new was happening without a predetermined outcome. While charismatic renewal has not delivered within Catholicism what it hoped for and at times claimed, it was an important stage in heralding the breaking down of some of the manufactured divisions between clergy and laity. One long-term consequence of this has been that lay people are increasingly less inclined to accept an institutional answer without adequate proof and justification.

Allied to this is the change whereby priests are no longer the only theologically qualified people in parishes. The decline in vocations for clergy and missionary orders resulted in various

Catholic educational institutions opening up third level theological study to lay people. Today literally hundreds of lay Catholics study theological issues at master's level and beyond. The days when the priest could speak without fear of contradiction have gone and more lay people than clergy are studying theology in contemporary Ireland. At times this study is deliberately ecumenical, further challenging the hold of the denominational Church as institution. A partnership between the Methodist Edgehill College (Belfast) and the Roman Catholic Mater Dei Institute (Dublin) has been teaching a part-time Bachelor of Theology degree to groups of lay Catholics and Methodists. Educated lay Catholics are taking an increasing role in the spiritual life of parishes, even if this is not as a Church policy. Church control on the teaching of the faith to the faithful cannot be maintained in this new era where there are increasing opportunities for study in many different ways and at many academic levels.

The reality may be that there is relatively little theology studied by today's clergy, especially beyond seminary training. Within the Catholic orders there has been a post Vatican II move from contemplative to pastoral roles. This was initially a theological understanding of their developing role and in recent years has become a pragmatic response to the declining numbers of parish clergy. Lay people have been taking up the task of theological reflection, formerly undertaken by these orders. In some ways this is how it should be. Clergy have normally had a number of years of theological study but surely they are not to be a religious elite who hold on to the mysteries of the faith, or seek to maintain the mystery of faith in the minds of the faithful. Clergy are pastors who seek to lead people into a mature faith. That this is starting to happen in unplanned ways is all part of the wonder of what God is doing in spite of the Church in contemporary Ireland.

The ministry of the Church is slowly being opened to lay people and women. Today lay people increasingly serve on mission teams that engage in short term mission projects within parishes. Lay people are entrusted with bringing communion elements to the elderly, housebound and ill as extraordinary ministers of the Eucharist and altar boys have been supplemented by altar girls. While these gradual developments are important in themselves and show a belated development of the spirit of Vatican II, they also point to further possibilities. They do not have to point to further specific developments, rather an understanding is developing that what was taken for granted as Catholic practice in the past need not be assumed to be unchangeable. This mindset, akin to a non-Anglican Protestant approach, creates the environment in which change and development is expected. The Church is changing and will increasingly allow itself to do so.

All these developments point to a change in an institution and in themselves do not point to the end of the institution. Indeed, many point to the continuation of an institution in a refined and renewed way. Yet, taken in total, they point to the end of a clerical, male dominated, hierarchical structure; that many of these changes are accidental points to the lack of willingness of the institution to become a movement. This is especially seen in the way the Catholic Church has dealt with returning missionaries. Many Irish missionaries have chosen to remain in retirement where they served, cared for by the church they helped to develop. Those that returned to Ireland, instead of being welcomed as returning 'heroes', found themselves initially disadvantaged over their pension rights, albeit more a technical detail than the state not willing to recognise appropriate the contribution these women and men have made in the name of Ireland. What the Church has not done is sought to fully understand from these returning priests and nuns what the insights of their ministry, often in places where Christianity is a small disadvantaged minority, can bear on a changing Ireland. Most of these missionaries are returning to a very different Ireland than they left. Those who departed in the 1950s and 1960s left a struggling Ireland with a vibrant Church. They have returned to a vibrant Ireland with a struggling Church. Many of them have far more experience of a struggling Church than the current leadership of Irish Catholicism. The missionary experience of how to work in a context where it is a disadvantage to be an active Catholic, where the state distrusts your motives, where obstacles can be placed in the way of your social ministries, where there are many competing spiritual choices before people and where clergy can be particular targets of physical attacks has been the reality for many of these missionaries. Much of this contribution is not currently being asked for or listened to.

Protestant Church

The beginnings of Irish Protestantism are hard to determine. While Henry VIII's desire for the Papal revenues from England, the wealth of monasteries and a change in his marriage situation did impact Ireland, it was the various plantations of Ireland with nominally Protestant English, Scottish and Welsh settlers that was the effective beginning. The fortunes of the Anglican, Presbyterian and Methodist denominations in Ireland have risen and fallen through a wide variety of issues, many of their own creation. What has been consistent in the Republic of Ireland has been the decline of these denominations since the creation of the state until the last years of the century. This was as the result of the decline in a British orientated population allied to a dominant Catholic Church and the effects of *Ne Temere* legislation negatively impacting the Protestant communities.

The arrival of both asylum seekers and economic migrants to Ireland from the late 1990s onwards has brought a significant number of new members for the Methodist and Presbyterian churches and, to some extent, the Church of Ireland. The Irish census recorded the Methodist community as approximately 5,000 in 1991 and 10,000 in 2002. While Methodism has not noticed a doubling of membership almost all individual congregations in the Republic of Ireland are recording increasing attendance. A number of Methodist congregations, such as in Abbey Street (Dublin), Galway and Killarney currently have a majority of non-Irish members. This increase in membership has been very welcome to individual congregations, many of whom were struggling to survive. A second factor is that many of these newcomers were formerly members of these denominations or ones similar. Many were already Worship Leaders, Lay Preachers and Sunday School teachers and the Irish Protestant denominations have had an influx of talented members. Other smaller or more independent Irish denominations have witnessed comparable growth and there has been a similar, although less marked, experience in Northern Ireland. While this growth is clear, the implications for mission in Ireland are not so obvious. This issue will be considered in chapters Six and Seven.

Does this growth change institutions into a movement? By itself, no; indeed such growth would normally suggest a strengthening of the institution. But it is the nature of this growth that challenges the institution. New members, often from a more vibrant or at least different background, challenge the existing institution. Traditional Irish ways of doing and being church have not been notably successful in the last generation and that is further questioned by an influx of people for whom the Irish way of doing things has not been their experience. The increasing involvement of such people in leadership positions means that the institution is forced to look at itself again. Whether this leads to dramatic change is yet unclear, but the possibility is now present. It may be that because this new challenge to the existing ways of being church is occurring during an era of growth, the denominations have the luxury of a relatively strong position and can act courageously rather than defensively.

A direct challenge to these institutions comes from finance. The traditional denominations rely on income from individual congregations to finance 'head office' staff. In recent years these central staff numbers have been increasing. Increasing legislation related to youth and children's work and financial administration has resulted in the creation of posts and increased training is being offered to people working at all levels within congregations. This is not yet a major problem to the Irish denominations in the way it is for their British equivalents. In the Church of England the first decade of the twenty-first century has witnessed the virtual cessation of new appointments in a number of dioceses for financial rather than personnel reasons. In early 2007 British Methodism announced that approximately one third of its head office staff positions would have to go in the next year while the United Reformed Church and the Salvation Army both are at risk of collapse as national denominations. Irish Protestantism is currently more robust than its British

66

equivalents but is heading in the same direction. The financial collapse of an institution does not automatically lead to the birth of a movement, but does point to that possibility.

In 2002 the Church of Ireland and the Methodist Church signed a covenant that while not guaranteeing unity did state the two denominations' desire to work closely together wherever possible. This sort of approach is to be expected when institutions are struggling. Closer working relationships, with the logical outcome of such a process being unity, can be viewed as an attempt by two struggling organisations to rationalise their operations, close individual churches where there is a dup-lication and reduce overheads. As such this is an attempt to sustain the institution but it does point to perceived weaknesses. These two institutions are clearly aware of their weakening position, at least in terms of their existence as institutions.

Among the denominations Irish Methodism is showing signs of recognising the problems of being an institution. Under a process called 'Connexions' Irish Methodism has been looking at its structures and seeking to reduce administration, do away with many of the committee meetings that are traditionally needed to sustain a Protestant denomination and create a much lighter and looser structure. This is an ongoing process that so far has been largely tinkering with the administration of the denomination. It may lead to more radical change, such as the recent decision to begin a process to do away with a district (similar to diocese) structure. Part of the argument was that this form of administration was simply not needed. Is this a pointer to Methodism as a movement? Or is it another sign of an institution struggling to keep itself going? Methodism should find it easier than most to contemplate a future as a movement as it began as a revival movement within Anglicanism before eventually developing into a denomination.

New Denominations
The Republic of Ireland has witnessing a flowering of a number of new Protestant denominations over the past fifteen years. In most towns and cities there is now a congregation that may call itself something like 'This Town Christian Fellowship'.

Within such a congregation almost all the members and leaders will come from a Catholic background but have entered into a new Christian experience that caused them to break with Catholicism but not to wish to associate with traditional Irish Protestant denominations. This makes sense when Catholicism is viewed as a cultural as well as a religious designation. In these congregations GAA shirts, Nationalist/Republican political views and an anti-British outlook can be found in a way unusual for other Irish Protestant congregations. Becoming a Protestant in Ireland used to carry a great deal of cultural baggage. This form of church is one attempt to embrace much of the experience of Protestantism without taking onboard the broader culture and tradition of Protestantism. These congregations deserve the designation of 'Protestant' due to their offering an alternative form of Christianity to Roman Catholicism and to their shared membership, with most of the historic Protestant churches, of the Irish Evangelical Alliance (EAI). This body is itself a response to the emergence of these new congregations. The Irish Council of Churches, as the representative body for historic Protestantism across Ireland, was perceived as a fairly static representation of the Protestant institutions. The EAI is a more fluid and diverse grouping.

The second, new grouping is of ethnic or mono-cultural congregations of which the most obvious examples are African denominations but also includes Eastern European and Asian groups. Within a few years the African denominations have numerically surpassed some of the smaller traditional Irish denominations and become a vibrant addition to the Irish Christian context. While a number of these appear to be very independent in outlook, some are actively involved with other local Christian groups.

The mere existence of the now numerous Protestant denominations in Ireland challenges the place of the Presbyterian Church and the Church of Ireland as the dominant Protestant institutions. These two denominations, formerly having a virtually unrivalled place within the Protestant community in their areas of influence, now find themselves jostling for position among the multitude of competing voices.

The main Protestant denominations are witnessing a small decline in people offering for ministry. This would be a major problem if it had not been for the decision by the Presbyterian and Methodist Churches in the 1970s to accept women into their ministry, followed in the 1980s by the Church of Ireland. A greater flexibility of ministry, including categories of ordained minister who work part-time in their local area without drawing a salary, means there is not a major problem, although the Church of Ireland is starting to struggle to maintain its parish system in rural areas of the Republic of Ireland. A further alleviation of this personnel issue has come through the recruitment of clergy from Britain, the USA and other English speaking areas. This said, the variety of clergy now found in these denominations has helped to loosen the institutional grip of the denomination. Not all Anglican clergy are trained in the same college, not all Presbyterian ministers are Irish, the local Methodist pastor might be an ordained women working part-time without a salary. These denominations now have a greater variety of clergy than ever before, many of whom do not have the loyalty to the institution of their predecessors who were of a more mono-chrome nature.

The many smaller denominations have a variety of responses to the issue of clergy. Many do not have ordination, others do not require a period of formal training, some use leadership teams which avoid the need for salaried pastors meaning there is little problem over leading and shepherding the flock for most of the smaller Protestant denominations.

Not every Christian institution is in decline. Relatively new institutional denominations, such as the Free Presbyterian Church, illustrate this. Yet their growth and that of other very conservative denominations has levelled off, if they have not started to decline. The upsurge in church planting of this movement peaked around the early 1980s, now a generation ago. It is increasingly apparent that while such traditional forms of Christianity still add a few members through the transfer of disaffected Anglicans, Presbyterians and others (the normal source of their membership) there is little missional impact on contemporary society. These conservative denominations have been largely a rural phenomenon. Their urban equivalents are the Pentecostal congregations and these have shown a membership as likely to have come from outside a believing Christian background as from transfer from other denominations. Their missional impact on society is deeper and likely to be longer lasting.

Within Britain and North America the phrase 'Emerging Church' is starting to become relatively well known. This new form of doing and being church will be considered in later chapters but it signals a willingness to re-imagine local congregations in ways that are radically different. Having a traditional church building, or even any building, is no longer essential. The day and time of meeting can be variable, as can whether that is weekly, monthly or as and when members think it worthwhile. Church might be cell or home based, might meet in a restaurant or hotel or be based on networks rather than geography. This has many implications for the future of Christianity but again points to part of that future being as a movement rather than an institution.

There has been one surprising development for Irish Protestantism. On the island of Ian Paisley and Orangemen it is becoming 'cool' to be Protestant; well, as long as it is at least fifty miles south of the border. It is largely through the efforts of Bono and most of U2, with as supporting act Graham Norton (and perhaps even a walk on part by one of Ireland's more colourful and harmless politicians, Senator David Norris) that has brought about this change. In the Republic of Ireland Protestants are being perceived as people of imagination and culture. Neither Bono nor Norton are representatives of mainstream Protestantism, although Bono habitually brings his faith into the public arena. The nature of cultural Protestantism is changing. Rather than the sombre, respectable farmer or small businessman, the Protestant can be perceived as imaginative, creative and a representative of the present and future Ireland, rather than its past.

Conclusion

So, is Christianity changing from an institution to a movement in Ireland? As society changes it is necessary for the Church to adapt. If this challenges the institution to become a movement, it is not clear whether the institution can successfully meet the challenge. Yet this chapter has argued that Christianity is at least showing signs of changing into a movement, even if most of these changes are being forced upon the Church.

Christianity as a movement in Ireland has not yet been born but the argument here is that this is the direction it is moving in. If this is the case, this is a change from what Christianity has been for most of the last 1500 years. Despite much of Protestantism historically developing into institutions by accident as much as by design, it may well be that Catholicism is showing more signs of becoming a movement, despite its reluctance to move in this direction.

If Christianity is exhibiting signs of institutional decline and developing at least aspects of a movement, this is largely accidental. Could a perspective that intentionally seeks to transition to a movement be effective? The Methodist 'Connexions' process is one example of such an attempt but has really only sought to streamline the institution rather than challenge its very being. In the early 1990s in Britain, the Assemblies of God denomination deliberately sought to transform itself from a congregational based system to a cell focused movement in response to decline, (what such a cell based system might look like will be considered in later chapters). This has been partially successful but points to the possibility of a denomination facing up to this issue.

If the Christian movement were to successfully develop out of the collapse of Christendom in Ireland, there is nothing to stop it attempting to rebuild institutional Christianity, although the last 1300 years of Irish Christian history should act as something of a caution. Yet this is hardly the place where the Church is at. The decline of the institution could herald the end of Christianity in Ireland. Fears as to how any movement might progress are a luxury that Irish Christians cannot presently enjoy.

In order for there to be any future for Christianity in Ireland an effective missional engagement is necessary and the following three chapters consider the issues involved.

1 In your experience, what are the advantages or disadvantages of Christianity as an institution?

2 Does a church need clergy?

3 Can you imagine one united Church in Ireland? What might it look like? What makes this difficult?

Chapter Five:

Twenty-First Century Mission

Mission has become an 'in-word' in Christian thinking. Rarely a Church statement comes out today without it being 'missional' in some way. While this means there is an increasing interest in the area of mission there is the resultant danger that almost anything that the Church does today is conceived of as mission. If everything is mission then nothing is mission.

Finding an agreed definition of mission is problematic as there are many different understandings of what mission means. For some there is the idea of a Victorian adventurer/missionary hacking his way through the jungle followed by a long line of native bearers carrying the innumerable 'essentials', often including his wife. For others it is a priest in a mission compound in Africa complete with school, clinic, church and parochial house, all surrounded by a substantial wall. Such a picture might be quaint and sepia tinted. The reality today is more likely to be stark and related to work in an inner city housing estate or involved with asylum seekers. In soteriological terms mission has been conceived as saving individuals from hell; ecclesiologically it was the expansion of the Church; culturally it was spreading the blessings of Christendom with all and sundry. So what does mission mean?

Rather than attempt one overarching definition Donal Dorr offered a number of 'mission as ...' headings in *Mission in Today's World* (Dublin: Columba, 2000), an approach that followed David Bosch in *Transforming Mission* (Maryknoll: Orbis, 1991). Andrew Kirk, a British Anglican in *What is Mission?* (London: DLT, 1999) suggested that:

> The theology of mission is a disciplined study which deals with questions that arise when people of faith seek to understand and fulfil God's purposes in the world, as these are demonstrated in the ministry of Jesus Christ. It is a critical reflection on attitudes and actions adopted by Christians in pursuit of the mission-

ary mandate. Its task is to validate, correct and establish on better foundations the entire practice of mission.

Historically mission was 'the mother of theology'. However, in keeping with an Irish contextual approach, I will be using the definition of the Irish born scholar Chris Wright, in his excellent *The Mission of God* (Nottingham: IVP, 2006). Unpacking the implications of the mission principles contained in this, forms the basis of the rest of this chapter. The study of mission or missiology is reflection on the practice of mission. It can never be ivory tower speculation and remain authentically missiology. Therefore the two subsequent chapters will offer concrete examples and insights as to how mission can be done in the Ireland of today and tomorrow.

Wright argues that mission should be understood as:

> our committed participation as God's people, at God's invitation and command, in God's own mission within the history of God's world for the redemption of God's creation.

This perspective, combined with Dorr's argument, helps to highlight a number of themes that form an authentically Christian, twenty-first century missiological understanding.

Missio Dei

Traditional understandings of mission, despite their many varieties, normally had one constant aspect; mission was what the Church did on behalf of God. The Church was God's instrument for 'doing stuff' on earth and the Church got on and did it. The missionary Church was related to God. However, missiological thinking in the last generation or two has attempted to reverse this order and understand that it is the God of mission who has a Church rather than the Church who carries out the mission of God. The Church is still integral to God's mission in the world but it is God's mission, not the Church's mission; hence *missio Dei.*

In the International Missionary Conference (which later merged to become part of the World Council of Churches) at Willingen, Germany in 1952 delegates started to articulate an understanding of mission as originating within the very nature of God. Therefore, God the Father in sending the Son, and God the Father and Son in sending the Spirit demonstrated the missionary nature of the Triune God. This was expanded to include the Triune God sending the Church and so the Church was dependant on God for its purpose. Church existed because of mission rather than mission occurred because there was a Church. Vatican II incorporated this ecumenical Protestant thinking into mainstream Catholicism in *Gaudium et Spes*.

The logical development of this concept is that the God of mission uses the Church in mission but is not exclusively bound to the Church or limited to the Church. The triune God is bigger than the Church and so the Church comes to be understood as God's chief, but not only or final, instrument of mission. This can lead to an idea that mission is God's work irrespective of whether the Church participates and so the Church is relegated to a virtually passive role, observing and supporting what God is doing but not being essential. The analogy of the spectators at a football match might be apt. They certainly assist their team, but their absence would not make the match invalid nor impossible for their team to participate in and even win. Therefore, is the Church useful but not essential to God's mission?

Part of the answer to this issue is to look at how God has worked in history. From a Scriptural perspective it is clear that God's people, be they Israel or the New Testament Church, have been central to God's purposes. But what is equally clear, although not always recognised, is that God has been at work among people outside of the chosen few. The people of Israel were chosen for a purpose but, as Amos 9:7-8 illustrates, other peoples were also chosen, albeit for a different purpose. When God laments for the sin and waywardness of Israel, He does something similar for the other tribes displaying a similar relationship (Jeremiah 48:31-32; Isaiah 15:5, 16:11; Ezekiel 30:1-5, 32:2, 27). Israel will be eventually restored, but then so will others (Isaiah 19:18-25; Ezekiel 29:13, Jeremiah 48:47, 49:6, 39). If God was only at work in the people of Israel how did

Nebuchadnezzar have a relationship with Him (Jeremiah 25:9, 27:6-7, 43:10)? What about Cyrus (Isaiah 44:28, 45:1), Jethro (Exodus 3:1, 18), Melchizedek (Genesis 14:18, Psalm 110:4, Heb 7:11) and even Job? Malachi declares that, in his day, God was currently receiving the praises of the nations (Malachi 1:11). What becomes clear from even a cursory rereading of the Old Testament is that a theological understanding that God was at work exclusively through the people of Israel in the pre-Christian era is untenable. The Bible tells other stories of how God was in different relationships with various peoples. The relationship with Israel was unique with regard to salvation and the coming of the Messiah. But there were other relationships also.

Is this maintained in the New Testament? Does the coming of Christ dispense with some of the ambiguity of the Old Testament? John's gospel builds up a picture of the Spirit at work where He wishes (John 3:8), that this work and truth is available to all people (John 1:9) and that God can be authentically worshipped by many (John 4:2). Among the Gentles faith can be found; for example among the Canaanites (Matthew 15:21-28) the Romans (Luke 7:1-10).

The two classic passages in respect to the work of God among others in the New Testament are the story of Cornelius (Acts 10-11) and Paul in Athens (Acts 17). The Gentile Cornelius is clearly a person who is in relationship with God, and God recognises Cornelius' prayers and worship. Cornelius can discern when it is God speaking to him, even a little quicker than Peter, and it is the apostle who needs a conversion experience before he can meet with the Gentile. Where has Cornelius' relationship come from? That it is not necessarily a saving relationship is not the main issue here (although it is a profound issue in a Christian understanding of the relationship of Christian faith to other faiths). God is at work in Cornelius' life prior to the meeting with Peter. This may be partially accounted for in Cornelius' status as a 'God fearer' in at least an association with the Jewish people although Cornelius had also not chosen to convert to Judaism. Whatever the level of his involvement with God's covenant people, the same message, from a different perspective, comes through in the encounter between Paul and the Athenians.

Paul is able to recognise that the Athenians are people of genuine religious interest. They are worshippers of many forms of divinity including one that Paul recognises as being the Triune God, even if to the Athenians this God is the 'unknown god'. Paul is able to affirm truth in the Athenians corpus of philosophical and religious writings and build on an already existing relationship with God. Once more in this encounter it becomes clear that this is not a full and complete or saving relationship with God. Some reject this new message but there are a small number of converts. The inter-faith significance of this is considerable in that it is possible to be in a genuine relationship with God but still need to move to a saving relationship. The point is clear that outside of the Jewish dispensation the Athenians have knowledge of the Triune God, are in a relationship with Him and are offering worship to Him.

So, what does this brief scriptural overview tell us about the *missio Dei*? There is confirmation of this concept in that Scripture tells a story of people who have knowledge of God outside of the direct work of the people of God in Israel or the Church. God is not limited to His people in His work on earth. Yet in both the story of Cornelius and that of Paul in Athens, where there is clear affirmation of a pre-existing awareness of God before the representative of the Church turned up, there was not a prior saving relationship. That was still needed. The Biblical and missiological affirmation is that God is not limited to His Church in order to work in the world, but the Church is the custodian of the saving truth of what God has done in Jesus Christ and that is an essential message for the world. Consequently, the Church in Ireland is essential to God's mission, but that mission is not limited to the Church.

Mission as Being

The early Church knew all about mission as being. Wherever they went and whatever they did, they existed in an environment that was hostile to Christian belief and practice. Simply existing as a Christian was to be missional. Stephen, a deacon rather than an apostle, was still arrested and martyred for sharing his faith (Acts 6:1 – 7:60). The subsequent major persecution resulted in the scattering of the early church and the spreading of the Christian faith. It was the natural way of life for these first Christians to share the story of Jesus, such as in the account of Philip in Samaria (Acts 8: 4-8) and with the Ethiopian Eunuch (Acts 8: 26-40).

Christianity spread more by the missional lifestyle of ordinary believers than by planned 'missions'. The spread of Christianity to Rome before the visit of Paul is but one example of this. Converted soldiers being moved about the empire and business people such as Lydia from Philippi (Acts 16:11-15) travelling for commerce were among the normal means of spreading the faith. The faith was transmitted by the missional lifestyle and speaking the name of Jesus by these 'laypeople' far more than organised missions by the Church hierarchy. Even a superficial stripping of the layers of legend associated with Patrick reveals Christian faith present in Ireland before the organised and officially sanctioned 'mission'. This was the norm.

Under Christendom the understanding of mission changed from what defined a follower of Jesus to the activity of specific religious professionals. The Christendom mindset was that everyone in a Christian society was a Christian and while there might be good Christians and bad Christians, all were still Christian. Mission eventually became what professional Christians did on behalf of the Church to engage with those on the fringes or beyond the faith. There were 'Mission to Jews', 'Foreign Missions' (eventually) and by the last century or so of Christendom the recognition of the need for 'Home Mission'. With the missionary movement from the sixteenth century onwards the concept of mission solidified into something that was done 'over there' by 'us' to 'them'. As the centuries progressed mission was normally considered as something that certain Christians did. Mission was important, some did it on behalf of the rest and life went on as normal. Christendom changed the early Christian understanding of mission and it is only with the collapse of Christendom that this misunderstanding of mission, as something some did, has started to be challenged.

Many non-conformist groups exemplified this approach. Being non-conforming voices under various forms of Christendom placed these people, if not always on the margins, at least away from the centre of power and influence. An example might be the early Methodists in Ireland. Converted through the ministry of John Wesley and his followers in eighteenth century Ireland, this small community never had the establishment status of the Anglicans or the numerical strength of Catholicism. Many of the converts were what might be described as 'upper working class' – hard working individuals who did not normally have the advantages of wealth or the ownership of significant land or property. These small farmers, shopkeepers and non commissioned officers in the British army simply lived a Christian lifestyle and participated in religious meetings and small groups to the extent that the wider population very clearly identified them as different. Persecution by Anglican gentry or a Catholic mob (often the two working together) was commonplace in the early days of this movement and a tablet in Moy Methodist Church, Co Tyrone com-memorates a lay Methodist preacher who died of his injuries inflicted in such an attack. The informal witness or missional lifestyle of lay people was largely responsible for the growth of Methodism. In the USA Methodism began in New York through the witness of Irish Methodist emigrants, the cousins Barbara Heck and Philip Embury from Ballingrane, Co Limerick, and in Maryland through the preaching of Robert Strawbridge of Drumsna, Co Leitrim.

A related way by which Methodism was spread was through the Christian witness of individual British soldiers. The story was usually something like this. An English soldier may have come to faith through the influence of a local Methodist in England and now found himself stationed in Ireland. The soldier, who had stopped drinking and gambling, would be promoted to sergeant as he was now recognised as increasingly trustworthy and diligent and he would gather a small group of interested soldiers around him in a small regular devotional meeting, often augmented by members of the local population. The regiment would be moved from Ireland to perhaps the West Indies and a small number of Irish people influenced by this soldier would be left behind to continue the Methodist witness. In the West Indies the sergeant would continue his religious interests. This would come to the notice of a few in the local community who would start to associate with the small religious group and when the sergeant was moved elsewhere a small Methodist community would be left behind again and so the story continued. So when Revd Thomas Coke, the first official Methodist missionary, arrived in the West Indies in 1784 he came to Antigua where there was a Methodist congregation of 1000 worshippers and a history that went back at least thirty years to the conversion of a prominent local called Nathaniel Gilbert. The Methodist community was led by a succession of lay people that included plantation owners, women and former slaves before the arrival of missionaries.

What does this have to say about mission in Ireland today? Rather than exciting strategies, innovation ideas and expertly trained practitioners, mission in Ireland needs saints and disciples. Saints in the Biblical sense of God's people who are called to a radically different, holy lifestyle; disciples who are learners of Christ who learn primarily by spending time with Him. Contemporary Ireland is awash with slick sales techniques and run by a plethora of ultra efficient MBA's. It does not have so many authentic saints and disciples and it is such as these who will stand out in local communities as different and be a missional presence and challenge simply by their very being.

Mission is part of what defines a follower of Jesus Christ. There are people who are the disciples of Jesus and those who are not. How Christians relate to those who are not Jesus' disciples is missional. While it includes evangelistic practices and strategies it is not confined to these. Every interaction with others is a missional moment. There may be opportunities lost, there may be poor witness given, disservice for Christ might well occur; such is the poverty of much of our faith and witness. But every encounter between a follower of Jesus and one who is not is missional. The early Church lived this. The challenge in the twenty-first century is to recapture this understanding and orientation of life.

Corporate and Individualistic Mission

A further implication of mission as being is that the locus of mission is principally located in individuals rather than in the Church as an institution. This is not to negate the corporate dimension but rather to reinterpret the Church as being primarily the association of people who are the followers of Jesus. Traditionally Catholic, Anglican and Orthodox ecclesiology understood the Church primarily in a corporate sense as a body to which individuals belonged. The hierarchy were the custodians and guarantors of the Church and people had to simply follow this lead. Under Christendom this made perfect sense. An alternative was exemplified in the ecclesiology of non-conformity that understood the Church to be primarily composed of individual congregations that themselves comprised the gathered community of believers related more in theological emphasises than through geographical proximity. Under this concept there were no parish boundaries and no inconsistency with having several congregations within a closely defined location to which individuals choose to belong to or otherwise. The collapse of Christendom and the development of post-modernity suggest this formerly non-conformist understanding of Church may well be becoming the only culturally viable model.

Rather than mission being the responsibility of the corporate body, the reinterpretation of the Church to be primarily the collection of believers logically places the missional task back onto those believers. Therefore all believers share this undertaking rather than some from the body being tasked with missional responsibilities. It is both good theology and post-modern necessity to understand the locus of mission being personal with the ecclesial role being supportive and enabling. Under Christendom the missional responsibility could be devolved to certain specific agencies. Today the role of those agencies is to enable the whole people of God to live out a missional lifestyle.

Mission to all creation

Built on an understanding of the *missio Dei* and mission primarily as something Christians are rather than do, mission is lived out in the world around us in a number of ways.

Evangelisation – The challenge to share the good news of Jesus in many ways with the hope and expectation that individuals will come to a saving faith in Jesus Christ is never absent, no matter what context Christians find themselves in. In Christendom this was largely through Christian education, in the parish or school, with the expectation that the latent faith within all baptised people would be raised and so lead to a genuine confirmation. The nominal faith so prevalent in Christendom was, of course, never the intention but pioneer evangelism was what missionaries did somewhere abroad. Once more this has all changed. The location for pioneer evangelism has returned to Ireland. Whatever your theology of baptism it is apparent that Christian faith is more likely to be absent than present in the lives of individual Irish people today. Hence the need for evangelism.

Evangelism is an appropriate approach to all people. The Christendom understanding of all in a community being within the fold of the Church is replaced by a similar universal concept but reinterpreted to view all people as within the orbit of God's love and grace. There is no-one who is beyond the scope of this evangelisation and no-one who cannot respond to such an evangelistic invitation. Equally there is no-one who does not need to respond to such a call.

Evangelism is undertaken by all as part of a missional lifestyle. It is not the area of a few trained professionals, orders or agencies. The decline in vocations in a number of Christian traditions, rather than a problem, is a helpful pointer to the vocation of the whole people of God to be evangelists. The New Testament picture of the early Christians is of a community that had a small number of individuals in leadership positions (a smaller number of whom were set aside for these tasks), and a few specifically appointed missionaries. But the picture is also of a missional community to whom the Lord added daily those

82

who were being saved. In Acts 2:42-47 the attractive picture given of the early church is primarily given in terms of the values and attitudes they held. By being such a community, the consequence was an increase in numbers. Their lifestyle was missional. They did not so much do mission as be mission, and it was demonstrably a successful missionary approach.

Poverty – It has become commonplace, both within Catholicism and ecumenical Protestantism, to speak of a Divine preferential option for the poor. That the Church, dazzled by the influence and prestige of Christendom, failed to see this for most of 1500 years is of lasting regret. Ireland still has a significant number of poor from traditional sectors, an increasing number who example relative poverty in relation to the beneficiaries of the Celtic Tiger, and the new poor who may include some of the recent immigrants to Ireland. There will be a future category of poverty yet to be understood, composed of the casualties of the Celtic Tiger resulting from a downturn in the economy and increase in house repossession. The Church's responsibility to the poor is an ever-present task.

Yet does this concept of 'a preferential option for the poor' hold up? It is certainly politically correct to argue this, and in the last generation this was an important corrective to the previous centuries. Was it an over corrective? If God has a preferential option for one section of the community this implies that other sections are considered in a less favourable manner. It may be that in the twenty-first century it is necessary to recover the understanding that God's love and grace encompasses all humanity, a concept that certainly includes the poor as one among many groups. The Irish Anglican author of the hymn 'All Things Bright and Beautiful' got it very wrong when she penned the verse 'The rich man in his castle, the poor man at his gate, God made them high and lowly, and order their estate'. I can remember singing that verse as a child and even then recognising that it just could not be right. It was a Christendom claim that had everything to do with bolstering the position of the traditional ruling elites and nothing to do with the gospel of Jesus Christ. An alliance between Church and state was always likely to accept such compromises.

There can be a captivity to Luke's 'blessed are you who are poor' (Luke 6:20) and a neglect of Matthew's 'blessed are the poor in spirit' (Matthew 5:3). The option for the poor has tended to interpret Luke in terms of economics and politics and the spiritual dimension of Matthew's call is lost. For a spiritual community the spiritual dimension needs to be paramount.

There is an increasing challenge in contemporary Ireland to look at mission among the rich, either the increasing number of wealthy in Irish society or the fact that the increasing prosperity of the nation has consigned the 'poor man of Europe' tag to a historic detail. If mission is to all, then it is to all sectors of society. We need to be fully aware that the spiritual vacuum at the heart of capitalism and wealth creation is an important area of Christian mission. Now that we are escaping the Christendom connection between wealth, power and the Church it is easier to raise this issue and challenge the idea of God having a preferential option. The Christian gospel empowers and challenges all. There is nothing in the gospel that exhorts wealth as God's desire for all, but equally nothing that sees poverty as a spiritually enriching experience. Poverty can certainly force an individual and a community to rely on God while material wealth encourages much of contemporary Ireland to rely on its own resources. Luke's words help us to view the poor as being in a blessed state, alongside various other sectors, but poverty in itself in not seen as a blessing. Christendom supported the wealthy and kept the poor in poverty. Post-Christendom can be an escape from all forms of oppression. Ireland has moved from an economically wealthy Church in a poor nation to a relatively poor Church in a wealthy nation.

Liberation – Mission must involve liberation. In Jesus' mission manifesto detailed in Luke 4: 14-30 He declares His role as to preach good news to the poor, freedom to captives, sight to the blind and the proclamation of the jubilee; a reminder that liberation is at the heart of the gospel. In 2007 the bicentenary of the abolition of slavery in Britain was celebrated. While Ireland is acknowledged to have had little direct involvement in the slave trade, indirectly Protestant Ireland benefited economically. Irish sea captains and investors did not bring

84

slaves from West Africa to the Caribbean and America. However, a number of Protestant businessmen engaged in supplying the goods and food required on many of the islands where a slave economy took hold. What often happened was that a small island, that formerly was virtually self sufficient in food for the relatively small population, changed completely under a slave economy. The whole island was given over to the production of one cash crop such as cotton or sugar cane, with virtually no food grown. The increased slave and settler population had to import almost all foodstuffs needed and this is where the Ulster Scots traders came in. Due to migration, many from this community had family ties to America and they proved adept at being the necessary 'middleman' between the Caribbean, America and Britain/Ireland. The ships that sailed from Belfast, Derry, Dublin and Cork did not carry slaves, but the prosperity of some of Ireland's business people was built on the trading associated with the slave trade.

Slavery still exists in many forms, even in Ireland. When the Garda Síochána raid a contemporary lap dancing establishment in Dublin the young women arrested/released generally are from Eastern Europe or Africa. Most have been 'trafficked', that is brought on pretext of other employment but on arrival in Ireland have had their passports taken by their 'advisors' and forced to work in the sex industry. There are perhaps more 'slaves' in Ireland today than in any other era of its history.

World economic systems, of which the Celtic Tiger is a major beneficiary, keep many developing world nations in a state that is akin to slavery. They are kept dependent on the cycle of development aid and only brought to a level of prosperity where they can consume western imports but not have the means to be an equal partner in the transaction. This system, whereby the western world gets comparatively richer, provides a steady stream of cheap labour to be absorbed in western economies. It is clear that the British health service has been built on the medical personnel of its Commonwealth. This is deplorable given the ratio of health professional to population in many of the countries that Britain has recruited from. It is not overly emotive to argue that Britain stays healthy because Africans and Asians die. A similar situation has been allowed to occur in the

Irish health system in the last ten years. In particular foreign nurses, who are usually from African or Asian countries with a much poorer health system to Ireland, are providing a significant amount of nursing care. Mission involves liberation and it is the role of the Church and individual Christians to be active in movements to bring fairness and equality. Anything less in sub-Christian.

Ecology – The world is well past the time when ecological issues were the interest of, if not a lunatic fringe, at least the mildly eccentric. The collapsing polar ice caps, the Alpine ski resorts that now only host hill walkers, flooding in Britain and the amazingly warm and pleasant Irish summers all point to the dramatic change in the world's climate. How does the Church respond to this? Christian mission occurs within the environment as entrusted to us by God and part of that mission involves the stewardship of this delicate ecosphere – something we have not been conspicuously successful at in recent generations. Ecological issues are missional issues and mission cannot be divorced from ecology. It is not just the backdrop to mission, a pleasant landscape on which to 'do' mission but rather the location of mission and the recipient of mission. The Christian's individual response to the environmental issues of the day is part of a missional lifestyle and Christian stewardship. It is not trite to say that many of 'the things to do', such as recycling, using low energy appliances and becoming carbon neutral are details that are essential in a missional lifestyle for individuals but also for Christian institutions.

Ryanair is one of the symbols of the Celtic Tiger, and equally symbolic of the ongoing despoliation of the environment by nature of its business as an airline. Imagine the carbon footprint of a Vatican III, if such an event were to be called. When the bishops of a national area make their five yearly visit to the Vatican, is that a good use of environmental resources? Do the seemingly endless committee meetings of the institutional Church need the expense of time, the environment and financial cost of face to face meetings or is a form of teleconferencing, now very commonplace and affordable, the missional way forward? In 2003-5 I co-authored a small book for the Bible Society with four others. We were all working in distant parts of

Ireland and to physically meet on a regular basis involved a cost in time and finance that was unrealistic. We met once at the beginning of the project as we were originally strangers to each other, again somewhere in the middle of the work and then near completion to consider the final drafts. Email contact was the main way we worked together at relatively little environmental cost. Physically meeting is still important; the incarnation is an example of the significance of this. Being able to put 'a face to a name' still works, and hopefully always will as relationship is an important aspect of Christianity that is increasingly important in postmodernity but conversely at risk of being lost in a technocratic world. But some of the ways we have 'done Christianity' in the past are not environmentally sustainable. It requires Christian individuals and institutions to do a lot more than change to low energy light bulbs. It requires a paradigm shift in thinking and lifestyle from an older generation and an acceptance of the mindset of a younger, more postmodern generation as the norm – in itself a humbling experience.

'Eco-Congregation Ireland' is an environmental programme for Irish congregations, supported by the Roman Catholic, Anglican, Presbyterian and Methodist Churches and based on a similar movement in Britain. Congregations are urged to go beyond the superficial replacement of light bulbs to audit every activity with regards to its ecological impact. It might involve the reshaping of church grounds, as exemplified in St Molua's, Stormont, Belfast. Dundrum Methodist church, Dublin has a drinks can lifting initiative where church members regularly go to local parks and communal areas to collect cans dropped as rubbish to take for recycling, both helping the immediate environment by the removal of rubbish and putting the aluminium cans back into circulation through recycling. Knocknagoney Parish, Belfast has hosted a 'Free Trees Campaign'. While such initiatives do not, on their own, make a significant impact beyond the immediate locality, this movement is designed to move churches from thinking of one off events to a mindset that puts ecological sustainability into all of its life as a community. As the Church is people this involves a change in lifestyle by the individual members as well as the corporate community activities.

Mission and Globalisation

That contemporary life is lived in a global world is apparent almost wherever you are on the planet. Finding a community that has never heard of Coca Cola is increasingly impossible, Starbucks coffee is drunk on every continent and more Guinness is brewed in Nigeria than in Ireland. The cities of the world are taking on a generic global appearance and the rapid spread of internet access is making 'to Google' a verb in a bewildering array of languages.

The Christian message is a worldwide message that seeks to counteract globalisation by becoming incarnate in every culture. Through translation Christianity takes a local root and then grows and develops as guided by the distinct local conditions. Globalisation needs to destroy the distinctiveness of different regions and reduce the world to one monochrome expression. While the Christian message seeks to reach all the world, today it has the confidence to allowing these local variations to thrive. Church architecture, clergy titles and clothing, worship styles and liturgies all reflect this diversity, all held together by the creeds and scripture.

In contrast Islam is a globalising religion. It shares with Christianity a desire to reach the world but Islamic expressions are more monotone. Arabic is the language of prayer and scripture wherever Muslims gather on the planet and local variations are often seen as heretical in some way or other. Of course, Christianity or at least Christendom has held similar views. When Francis Xavier reached India in the sixteenth century he was surprised to find Christians there, who were descended from the converts of St Thomas. His response was to seek to incorporate them within the practices of the Church he represented. Today, to find a Christian community with an unbroken and uninfluenced lineage going back to a disciple of Christ would be an incredible opportunity for the wider Church to learn from. Despite the relatively enlightened perspective of Xavier, the Thomian Christians were turned into good Catholics. The globalising dimension of Christendom, where there was uniformity and conformity within its boundaries, has been replaced by the more fluid 'world Christianity' where there are local, distinctive varieties of the Christian faith.

Mission as Doing

After all this, is there any doing left in mission? I have argued that mission is primarily being and the aspects of doing are first and foremost our authentically Christian responses to life situations rather than carefully worked out strategies and plans. This is a missional life and without this in action nothing else that Christians do will have much impact. An Irish generation has witnessed Church leaders saying one thing but allowing other practices to happen. There is a great need for authenticity. But within this understanding of the normal Christian life, there is still place for doing mission.

There are necessary times of specific missional focus in the life of a Christian community. There may be occasions when the events of the day call for a concerted response to an issue such as drug misuse or developing world inequality. Both in response to such events, and better still in a pre-emptive way, Christians will want to do things that highlight, more than normally, the Christian perspective on the issue. That this needs to be backed up by prior and subsequent lifestyle choices by Christians should not need to be repeated. Any idea of picking up an issue, shining a Christian spotlight on it for a while, and then dropping it back into the gloom again completely fails to be a Christian approach, even if such was an historic way of operation.

There will be occasions where a particularly focused evangelistic emphasis will be given. For example, it may be appropriate for a particular Christian community to view the long Irish summer school holidays as an opportune time to focus on a particular evangelistic approach to children and/or young people through running a 'Holiday Club' scheme. This does not imply that the social, physical and spiritual well being of children is not of concern to this community the rest of the year. But it does illustrate that it is still valid, and important, to plan for particular mission projects that are more conceptually doing mission.

There are missional principles that are authentically Christian responses to the gospel and the contemporary world. These need to be further interpreted for particular contexts and the following two chapters will interpret these principles for contemporary Ireland.

Questions

1   Does your church have a missional or pastoral understanding? If missional, how is it carried out?

2   Is it harder to be a Christian than to do a number of Christian activities?

3   How do you as an individual practically respond to ecological issues? How important is this area to you?

Chapter Six:

Being Missional in Contemporary Ireland

Mission is an expression of Christian individual and community life. It is being before it is doing. Without the aspect of being, any missional activities become divorced from an authentic expression of Christian community, or Church, and become meaningless exercises. However, Irish Christians need to remember that they are not the prime agents of mission in Ireland, whether through being or doing. The Holy Spirit is at work in Ireland through the Church and beyond the Church. This needs to be a constant recognition that both empowers Irish Christians to know that being missional is done in the power of the Spirit and liberates them in that mission is not totally dependant on Irish Christians to fulfil.

There is a further level where the Church has always understood there to be specific times of revival during which the Spirit will move in a clear way to convict and convert individuals. The Patrician mission and the 1859 revival in Ulster may be two such examples. When such a time returns to Ireland the sovereign work of the Spirit will very probably dwarf all the combined endeavours of Irish Christians. Such a day will come, but there are no indicators that this day is imminent. This is not 'pie in the sky' but good theology. Mission is a time-limited occurrence that can be overwhelmed by the work of the Spirit and will cease at the return of Christ.

Therefore, based on the map of the changed Ireland that has been drawn in earlier chapters, taking into account the necessary missional understandings for contemporary life, and with recognition of the place of the Holy Spirit in mission, what specific principles of being missional need to be foundational for Irish Christians in the twentieth first century?

People of Fun

Far from superficial, I have deliberately put this first as this may be the biggest missional need today and the area where Irish Christians, in recent generations, have most spectacularly failed. Any caricature contains an element of truth, but not the whole truth. Rarely is there a caricature of Irish Christianity where fun is the chief element. Irish Christianity may be laughed at, but it is not often portrayed as a fun thing in itself. Whether it is censorious puritanical Protestants from the north, or a portrayal of Catholicism obsessed with repression, guilt and a penitential lifestyle, there is not much fun going on. 'Father Ted' was probably a great service to contemporary Irish Catholicism in that it allowed Catholics to laugh at their tradition in an age when that tradition was being scrutinised for far too many failings. Father Ted came along in an era when Irish society, emerging from Christendom, was just about free to look humourlessly at itself. If the programmes were to be made today, too many serious issues would crowd in to allow the relatively harmless portrayal of Ted, Jack and Dougal. The nearest Ulster Protestant equivalent may well be 'Pastor Begley' from BBC Northern Ireland's 'Give My Head Peace'. This shadowy figure is portrayed as little different to Protestant paramilitaries and above all is a figure to be obeyed and feared. Such was a partial role for Protestant clergy in Ulster's history. Irish Christianity, despite its Celtic life-affirming heritage, is rarely portrayed as fun, even if the Irish individual is often portrayed as a humorous character. A brief consideration of Biblical material will build a foundation for this approach.

Tax officials are presumably as humorous as anyone but society, past or present, has rarely considered them such. Therefore, when Matthew the tax official meets with Jesus and responds to the call to follow, his first action is to throw a party to introduce his old friends to this new community of the followers of Jesus (Luke 5: 27-32). It is quite a party, so much so that some Pharisees notice what is going on and complain about the breaking of religious purity barriers. When Zacchaeus meets with Jesus it is Jesus who calls for the party and Zacchaeus who shows his reckless generosity as a host – surely an appropriate response to Jesus (Luke 19: 1-10). In the wedding at Cana, when the party is starting to flag because of the lack of wine, Jesus performs a miracle that gets the party going once more in a far more extravagant way that was necessary (John 2: 1-11). Jesus breaks religious laws to affirm the spirit of the law rather than the letter (Mark 2:23-27). When the lost son returns to his father, the elder brother is unhappy over the generosity of the party to celebrate his return but this is in the context of the parables of the lost sheep and lost coin. When the lost is found scripture sees this as a time for rejoicing and so there is rejoicing in heaven over the repentance of sinful people (Luke 15: 1-32).

Perhaps the heart of this is found in the comparison of John the Baptist's disciples to the followers of Jesus. The Pharisees accept, to some extent, John's companions because they deny themselves most material comforts and carry out a rigorous programme of religious observance and asceticism. It also helps that John appears a bit strange in his clothing and food habits. Such is a recognisably religious group. However, Jesus and his community do not fit this pattern and so the Pharisees question Jesus because 'John's disciples often fast and pray, and so do the disciples of the Pharisees, but yours go on eating and drinking'. Jesus' answer is key. Because He, as the bride-groom, is present you cannot expect the guests to be gloomy although that time will come (Luke 5: 33-35). This was fulfilled at Calvary but the inauguration of the community of Jesus followers, the Church, as the bride of Christ allows this period of celebration to recommence and to culminate one future day when people of every tribe and tongue stand around the throne celebrating Jesus (Rev 7: 9-17).

Christianity as fun is not a trivial or superficial concept. It is an essential experience because so much of the stuff of life is miserable. It is because children get cancer; it is because the randomness of birth condemns too high a percentage of humanity to suffering, poverty and early death; it is because most of the last two hundred (and more) years of Irish history has included famine, violence, poverty and forced migration that there needs to a place where authentic enjoyment can be found that is life affirming and not damaging as too many forms of entertainment are. When the local priest in rural Ireland was running dances to encourage community life he was serving the purposes of God more than many recognised. If the two options are either a censorious authoritarian Church, or the fun loving community of people who love Jesus, it is not hard to think which is more attractive, and which is likely to have more missionally impact. The parish fête has too often declined into a half hearted car boot sale and only justified if it is raising funds for a worthy project. If it can be recaptured as a celebration of all that makes community, centred around the Christian people who experience this more than anyone else, then God is glorified. Irish Christians need to be increasingly people of fun.

People of Humility

In Christendom when Church leaders lived in palaces, had a plethora of titles that all pointed to their individual importance such as Lord Bishop and Very Reverend, had rings to be kissed and received tithes from the population, humility was rarely the dominant characteristic. The Pope had temporal control over the Vatican States until relatively recently and some English Anglican bishops still sit in Britain's House of Lords by virtue of their ecclesial office and exercise a subsequent political role. Clergy of other denominations who are currently in the Lords sit as political appointments rather than as Christian leaders. In post-Christendom, an attitude more akin to that of Christ is what is required.

Ireland has had enough of clergy exercising power both north and south. It also has had many examples of humble Christians but they, by nature of that humility, rarely come to prominence. A humble Church is one that understands its position as the gathering of the followers of Jesus Christ. This has nothing to do with political influence, wealth or prestige. It is about following a Saviour who called those who wanted to follow him to give up everything.

In a nation of increasing wealth, any wealth that the Church has is now only relative. There is nothing unique or enticing about this. Indeed quite the reverse. Wealth, as defined by the grandeur of buildings and their ornamentation, is both a Catholic and Protestant phenomenon. The pre-Reformation cathedrals retained by the Anglicans were followed by Catholic basilicas and in recent years this pattern has been continued in a number of major evangelical church buildings erected in greater Belfast such as Ian Paisley's 'Martyrs Memorial' complex and Whitewell

Metropolitan Tabernacle (probably Ireland's only 'mega-church'). The most impressive recent religious building in Ireland is probably the Islamic Cultural Centre and mosque in Clonskea, Dublin and it is not hard to see these various buildings as helping to provide a definition of a particular religious minority community as much as anything else. Many of Ireland's greatest ecclesiastical buildings were erected when that tradition was numerically in a minority or else in a relatively powerless position.

The time has now come for the followers of Jesus to recognise that Jesus' choice of a donkey rather than a stallion was a lifestyle calling. The temptation to mount the stallion has always been present and throughout Christendom it proved irresistible. Rather than the way of humility being accepted due to reduced circumstances, today it can be embraced as the authentic first choice of the Jesus community. This will need to be translated into every aspect of the life of God's people. Church leaders can drop some of their more exalted titles, or perhaps them all, and moderate their incomes and lifestyles to primarily reflect Jesus rather than the Church. Church buildings need not be a demonstration of power but rather places where authentic community is experienced and enjoyed. Having the ear of politicians should be an unusual luxury rather than a right demanded like a spoilt child who is no longer getting their way. Church leaders should be primarily seen at Christian community events rather than state events. Evangelism becomes an invitation to all to join the community rather than a rebuke to those who are lapsed and should know better.

Consequently, mission is undertaken with an understanding that Christians have no more right to share their faith understanding than anyone else. Christians humbly, although without apology, can share their experience of God in Christ with all without demanding the positions of privilege that Christendom afforded them. In state occasions Christian representatives now take their place alongside representatives of other faiths. Access to the media is understood in the same way. The privileged position of Christian education being largely financed by the state becomes understood as a responsibility rather than an opportunity to propagate a narrow denominational perspective. The symbol of the cross is a reminder to Christians of the calling to follow the path of Jesus. Such is the path of humility.

People of a Kingdom

For generations Christians have been held captive by partisan and political understandings of kingdom. Even if not all Irish Protestants considered themselves as unionist or Catholics as nationalist, it still worked as a generalised orientation and pointed to the difficulty of a people trying to serve more than one master. Christians are first and foremost people of the Kingdom of God. Any earthly kingdom is very much secondary. Under Christendom the Kingdom of God was interpreted as being virtually personified in the particular political state that the Church endorsed. Post Christendom this is untenable but it is taking a couple of generations to work this out.

This focus on the Kingdom of God orientates the Christian community to the values of this Kingdom rather than those of the political rulers of a local society. Justice, equality and love are values that the inhabitants of God's Kingdom seek to live out day by day. The political compromises and expediencies necessary under Christendom disappear when there is no political master to endorse. Allegiance to the state is secondary to allegiance to Christ.

Christians are also freed from the desire and temptation to attempt to rebuild Christendom. In recent elections in the Republic of Ireland, candidates standing on a platform of traditional Catholicism have done very poorly. Christendom and its legacy is a problem to be overcome rather than a history to emulate.

People of Community

Christians have always helped to create community. The institutions of local churches have been integral in building and defining local communities. As late as the 1970s large new housing estates would often have a piece of land set aside to be given to an appropriate denomination to build a local church – this seen as an essential component of creating an attractive community. The days of church events being community events have largely disappeared, at least in the towns and cities. Even the Christmas and Easter celebrations are not community focused in the sense of being 'owned' by the wider population. Many might attend, but it is in the role of spectators and consumers of a religious product.

Christians have retreated into a Church community, or it may be more accurate to say Christians have been abandoned by the wider community and while the believers think they are an integral part of the wider population the reality is that population has emotionally moved on. Such is life in the twenty-first century. The missional need is to re-engage with the wider community.

If there are evangelistic forays into the wider community with the hope of capturing a few new converts to bring back 'home' then this Viking approach to faith has little to commend it. In the incarnation, without a conscious effort, Jesus was one with his local community, and this to such an extent that he was known as the Nazarene. The twenty-first century task is for Christians to be a natural part of their community.

In some ways this is a harder lesson for Protestants. Evangelical Christianity has been, at least in the nineteenth and twentieth century versions, an activist faith where new members were introduced to a lifestyle where the weekly attendance at a couple of church services, a prayer meeting, perhaps a Bible study and leadership of a youth or children's group was normal. When this activity was added to the plethora of committees – not all of which involved activism – then the week was full and the believer was congratulated on being an active and committed member of the church. The faith of the believer was shown by what they did rather than by who they were. When Church and society were synonymous under Christendom this was a busy life but at least one lived in the community. With the collapse of Christendom all this activism has become dislocated from the general community and located only within the faith community.

Such religious activism leaves little time for community involvement today. It is a brave evangelical who skips the prayer meeting or property committee meeting to participate in the local art club. How does the local congregation view the believer who coaches a Sunday morning soccer team? Is he or she a lapsed Christian? Or are they recognised as someone who has taken their faith beyond the confines of the believing community so that they can fully participate in the wider community, and so live out their missional life among people who are not followers of Jesus?

When congregations want to have a missional involvement in their wider community today, often the first task is to find points of contact in the various community organisations and clubs. How much easier is the doing of mission when Christians are being naturally missional by living the great majority of their life outside the Christian community? Time spent on cultivating wider relationships might be missionally more effective than many slick programmes that are attempted. The local church is not Noah's Ark, keeping safe the few from the destructive world outside. Rather the church is the upper room, where the faith community has gathered, but cannot stay within as the love of Jesus points them outside.

People of Faith

The Church is primarily a spiritual community and there are a number of tasks traditionally carried out by the Church that are now (better?) carried out by the State. Education, health care and social provision were tasks that the Church nobly undertook to better the lot of all. There were generations when the Church was the only institution where people of sufficient education, skill and commitment to serving others could be found and teaching and nursing were rightly considered to be vocations. Today the state has come of age and in a politically pluralist society it is inappropriate that state provision should be exclusively or largely undertaken by the Church as an agent of the state.

This is not to invalidate Christian education or health provision in the twenty-first century. The state may 'employ' Christian institutions to carry out certain roles, but the Church is acting in a supportive and subsidiary role. Christians may provide particular approaches to education or health care that their own community will want to avail of but that is as a choice rather than something funded by the national population. Indeed the Church might increasingly look to provide specialist services that the state and individuals may buy into. Specialised third level education is one example. But it is inappropriate today for the Church to provide general services that belong to the remit of the state.

The main point, however, is that the Church should be freed from much of the institutional provision of the past and at liberty to recognise its chief calling as a spiritual community rather than as a handmaiden to the state. For too many generations the Church was known for its social provision and its spiritual dynamic was hidden. This is the issue that starkly confronts the Salvation Army today in Ireland. As a provider of social services the Salvation Army continues to maintain an important and notable role. Yet a decline in membership and an aging faith community questions its ability to continue as a spiritual body much beyond 2020. Should it abandon its social care to attempt to rebuild its spiritual base? Probably not. The Church universal is composed of many traditions and callings and it is not the role of any particular denomination to encompass the whole Church, even if many have understood it that way. The Salvation Army is an excellent caring ministry of the Church Universal but its present state needs to be heeded as a warning. When the Church sees itself as anything other than primarily a spiritual community ultimately it will not continue.

If the Church devoted as much time, energy and expertise into its calling as a spiritual community, would it be in the present state of decline? It is easy to reinterpret history with the benefit of hindsight but the calling on the Church today is to be primarily a community of faith. Christians need to be noted as spiritual people who care for others, rather than community minded people who are also religious.

People of Influence
A reinterpretation of the Church as primarily a movement can imply that the Church becomes an inward looking and self-absorbed community. If this were to happen, it would be as much a denial of the ministry of Jesus as Christendom was.

Christians need to be at least as active in the world around them as ever, but as committed lay people engaging in the political and social institutions rather than as a hierarchical organisation. The smaller Protestant denominations and other religions in Ireland have been able to influence Irish society through individuals rather than through their own structures. Whether it is Jewish politicians or Presbyterian academics, it is individuals of faith making a difference and impacting wider society.

However I am not advocating a withdrawal from public issues. Indeed, Christian influence should increase rather than diminish. Christians should always want to influence society with Christian values but in postmodernity an appeal to traditional authority will prove ineffective. Christians need to earn the right to influence society rather than expect positions of power. It may be harder for Christians in some areas to rise to prominence. So be it. Christians call for fairness for all and equality as a social standard, but are also fully aware that to be a disciple of Jesus involves taking up the cross in order to follow.

People of Evangelism

One consequence of the modern society we are now leaving behind is a reliance on programmes for much of church life. Whatever the issue there is a course to follow, a book to read, and a programme in which to participate. The sharing of faith, or evangelism, has been captured by this climate as much as anything else. A consequence of this is if Christians use programmes in evangelism then the sharing of faith becomes something that is done rather than something that naturally flows from a person. Rather than empowering, this programme-orientated approach has had the opposite effect. Creativity in local congregations has been stifled and a managerial model followed whereby the implementation of a predetermined strategy is considered the way forward. Commerce and industry have been allowed to dictate the aims and methods of the Church and the transmission of faith has been unhelpfully 'professionalised'. The individual responsibility and response to an immediate local community or network needs to be recreated to be effectively evangelistic.

There is a natural sharing of faith that Ireland's Christians need to rediscover. It involves a lifestyle that unconsciously portrays the values of Jesus. This, in itself, is evangelistic in that it is truly counter cultural. In a wealth-orientated nation, a lifestyle that clearly follows a different pattern of priorities is literally remarkable. Yet this needs to be backed up with the ability to naturally articulate something of the story of Jesus. If the current trend to invite someone who shows interest in Christianity to a programme in the church, parish centre or local hotel, then faith sharing is reduced to a impersonal formula and divorced from the context that created initial interest. Evangelism needs to be rescued from something Christians do to something Christians are.

In this chapter a number of missional attitudes have been articulated. In some of these areas Irish Christians have not been traditionally successful. In other areas Irish Christians have been captured by a managerial and institutional approach that was appropriate for a certain era but that time has now largely gone. Being missional in a way that engages with twenty-first century Ireland is an essential foundation before any 'doing' of mission makes sense. With this understanding the doing of mission, that supplements and is secondary to the being of mission, is considered in the following chapter.

Questions

1. How does your local church express the fun of Christianity? How might you do this more?

2. Are you as an individual intentionally evangelistic? Is your church?

3. How do you make a Christian voice heard in contemporary Ireland?

Chapter Seven:
Doing Mission in Contemporary Ireland

The following chapter considers contemporary mission from the perspective of what needs to happen rather than what is happening. This includes recognition of missional trends and developments that are occurring that need to be further developed.

Ecumenism

Ecumenism is a problem in Northern Ireland in a way shared by few other nominally Christian parts of the world. Generally conservative denominations that are not naturally inclined towards ecumenism, further complicated by tribal political identities, has meant that too often the denominations and their pastors have been chaplains to their own narrow community rather than prophets. The pastors supported their people in their lives but rarely challenged on issues related to their community. In a situation of conflict this could have been perceived as close to treasonable. Yet this is changing.

Fifty years ago there was little interaction between the various Protestant denominations. Presbyterians, Anglicans, and in a couple of pockets, Methodists were content within their own little versions of Christendom. Today there is a covenantal agreement between Anglicans and Methodists where the logical, although not inevitable, outcome is unity. The Anglicans and Methodists, and Presbyterians and Methodists have experimented with united congregations in a few places although some of these long standing arrangements have come under recent stress. Part of the reason for this ecumenical progress is an increased world-wide ecumenical spirit among the equivalent denominations but perhaps of greater local significance has been the growth of more conservative denominations such as the various Pentecostal churches, Free Presbyterian, Baptists and Independent Methodists. These alternatives, signs in themselves of the breakdown of Christendom, prompted the mainstream Protestant denominations to see points of common interest a little clearer. United services, pulpit exchanges, shared youth and children's work, joint evangelistic work and combined ministerial training are all normal today in a way that would have surprised earlier generations. I well remember my Presbyterian practical theology tutor who joked that he felt his ministry in Newtownards in the 1970s had been successful when he moved his congregation's thinking on 'mixed marriage' from it being a marriage between a couple from First and Second Presbyterian to a marriage between a Presbyterian and a Methodist. Are we coming closer to a time when a 'mixed marriage' will be defined in Ireland as that between a Christian and a Muslim?

In the Republic of Ireland ecumenism has moved forward with greater pace for a related reason. Vatican II gave a theological impetus to Catholicism to at least look more positively on Protestant denominations at the same time as declining Protestant numbers made the legacy of Anglican establishment and British orientation less threatening. The recent arrival of significant non-Christian populations has resulted in increased ecumenical understanding. Both Protestant and Catholic communities have to respond to this new situation and easily realise their common interests in relation to these new faith communities. Whatever differences Protestants and Catholics perceive between each other are dwarfed by the differences perceived between Christians and, say, Muslims. A beneficiary of this new awareness is ecumenism. The arrival of others has made the similarities between different forms of Christianity a lot more obvious.

The days of competing Christendoms are over and to be effectively missional today needs an ecumenical spirit. Too often Protestant denominations have seen evangelism as a way of improving their own local congregation and denomination. It was about gains for 'their' side. When a young couple were married it was expected that the couple would associate with the denomination of the husband but that form of denominational mentality has also gone. Mission needs to be about the Kingdom of God and an ecumenical spirit recognising it is the Kingdom of God that needs to grow and develop.

Too often ecumenism in Ireland has been motivated by weakness. Ecumenical co-operation only significantly developed when the Protestant denominations began to decline. It is not coincidental that the strongest Protestant denomination, the Irish Presbyterian Church, is the least ecumenical of the mainstream Protestants. The Presbyterians do not see a pragmatic need for ecumenism, given its background coming out of a weakened situation. Can ecumenism be re-imagined as a missional orientation? Is it possible for denominations and local churches to see that mission simply makes more sense and has greater opportunities when done with each other? Authentic ecumenism is not a distraction from mission but an enabling force within mission.

So, what does ecumenical mission look like? It might be that the three or four small local churches in a village or rural area join together in ongoing social projects. In doing this together they are creating possibilities that on their own would have been impossible. They are additionally overcoming the suspicion that organising the community 'meals on wheels' scheme is being done to somehow promote or benefit a particular local congregation. An ecumenical approach demonstrates that this is God's work to honour Him rather than a local congregation engaged in self-publicity. Or it might be that several congregations in a town unite to hold a series of evangelistic events. The combined numerical and financial strength enables them to host a team of young people who engage in picking litter, tidying up a local community and seeking to provoke conversations as to why they are doing this. A skilled contemporary evangelist can be employed alongside this to lead a series of events that in an attractive way engage various sectors of the local community. Once more there are no mixed motives involved and Christianity is seen in a united and positive light. Perhaps a combination of congregations or parishes might be able to employ a detached youth worker and provide a neutral venue from which to engage with local young people who have little real knowledge of or connection to the local churches except a vague negative reaction.

Ecumenical mission creates new possibilities and overcomes certain problems. Of course, it does create its own difficulties for the participants but these are worth working through. Such ecumenical mission is becoming relatively commonplace. It is good missional practice and orientation. Increasingly, poor missional practice will be even less effective in the future than at present.

Power to Change - An excellent example of ecumenical evangelistic work was the 2002 Power to Change campaign. Fully ecumenical committees in both Northern Ireland and the Republic of Ireland worked through a network of parishes and congregations of a wide variety of denominations to finance and participate in evangelistic events around a media campaign and distribution of DVDs of the Jesus film. This was a multi million pound exercise modelled on an earlier Canadian initiative and exemplified good mission practice by being ecumenical, learning from others, being imaginative and using contemporary media of DVDs, computers and TV advertising. Subconsciously this campaign acknowledged the post-Christendom context of Ireland as Christianity was portrayed an option to be considered rather than the obvious faith of the Irish and one to which lapsed Christians should return.

An unforeseen consequence was how this campaign managed to depict Christian faith as positively controversial. RTE blocked the broadcast of some of the associated TV advertisements on the grounds that they were promoting a religion. On a channel that happily broadcasts adverts for tarot readings, mainstream Christianity could not advertise anything close to an evangelistic message. The resulting controversy bought the campaign more publicity than it could ever have financed and revised adverts were eventually broadcast. While this exemplified the perhaps less than neutral position where Christianity now finds itself in today's Ireland, it also showed a fine contemporary missional approach. The campaign was not hugely successful in terms of people coming to Christian faith. It certainly had a level of success that was measured anecdotally rather than objectively but this very lack of overwhelming numerical response is one more indicator of the situation within which Irish Christians engage evangelistically and missionally.

Sectarianism

The issue of sectarianism has bedevilled Irish Christianity in general and especially in Northern Ireland for the last three or four generations. Groups of terrified girls being herded through lines of protesting loyalists to attend a Catholic primary school filled the TV screens in the early days of the twenty-first century. Not so visible were leaders of the two communities who, from their respective motivations, saw this as good publicity. In my home-town of Dungannon I well remember an IRA terrorist killed on active service being eulogised from the pulpit of the local Catholic church as someone who loved his 'family, faith and community'. The weapon found on his body had been taken in the murder of a lay preacher of the Methodist church. The sight of Orangemen in aggressive stance towards the Police Service of Northern Ireland against the backdrop of Drumcree Parish Church, Portadown has sadly become one of the iconic images of Northern Ireland. All this is the stuff of sectarianism.

It is the association of institutional Christianity with particular political and cultural causes that has been problematic. That Protestantism and Catholicism have not always been associated with the respective Unionist and Nationalist causes has been largely airbrushed from history. It is generally not celebrated in the nationalist movement that most of the early leadership were Protestants or in the unionist family to acknowledge the pivotal role of Protestants in the creation of Irish nationalism. It is equally overlooked that the United Irishmen of 1798 saw non-Anglican interests coalesce. Or that the Orange Order was an organisation created to defeat an anti-Anglican movement as much as it was to support a unionist agenda. That the Celts who came to be known as Ulster Scots found an alliance with their traditional enemies, the English, rather than with their fellow Celts, is one of the many lost opportunities of Irish history.

Sectarianism in the Republic of Ireland has been largely overcome through economic prosperity, the decline of institutional Catholicism, growth in the Protestant denominations but mostly through the arrival of non-nationals who have become a rather more different 'other'. While it would still be surprising for a non-Catholic politician to become Taoiseach, such an event is more likely than ever before. A Protestant Taoiseach would be no more surprising today than a conservative Catholic politician elected on a traditional Catholic agenda.

Despite recent political progress in Northern Ireland sectarianism still appears to have a significant hold and to be institutionally supported, despite the various denominations having programmes to tackle the issue. The informal links between the Orange Order and some of the Protestant denominations is a problem to many. The Catholic Church's involvement with the GAA, with its history of discrimination against those who served in the RUC or British Army, has similar connotations for others. Both these particular issues are becoming of less significance, although it was clear that the recent GAA move towards liberalisation moves had its main support from the Republic of Ireland rather than Northern Ireland. In 2007 a leading Fermanagh GAA player, who was a Protestant, stopped playing for a period citing abuse from other players and lack of support from referees as the main reason. His father, a UDR soldier, had been murdered by the IRA twenty-five years earlier. Memories are both long and cruel in Ireland.

Numerous institutional initiatives, pronouncements and policies have failed to solve this issue. How sectarianism might well be addressed, at least in one aspect, is through the decline of institutional Christianity that has been highlighted. The weakening of the denominations and official institutions of Christianity will lessen the link between organised Christianity and sectarianism. This in itself will not solve the sectarian issue. What it will do is take away one significant plank of legitimation that the denominations have, at times inadvertently, provided. Additionally, Christianity will no longer bear the disgrace of being associated with sectarianism and the violence that too often accompanies it.

Particularly in Northern Ireland, the two main branches of Christianity have acted as chaplains towards their respective communities. In many ways this is positive. There has been a close identification between church, clergy and people; there is an involvement in all aspects of community life and there is a strong pastoral support in the midst of a divided and all too often violent society. The sight of Fr Aidan Troy escorting small children to Holy Cross School in Ardoyne, Belfast, and the Protestant minister comforting a widow and children at the graveside of a murdered parishioner near the border are iconic images of this chaplaincy role.

Under such pressure, a prophetic role that challenges is difficult to maintain. The hurts are often too deep to hear the voice of God in the challenge of the prophet. The voice of the pastor is so much more comforting. But the pastoral voice tends to continue, to some extent, the status quo. To everything there is a season and Northern Irish Christianity should be rightly proud of the pastoral role it played, even if there was at times an over identification with a particular political cause. There were individual prophetic voices. In the relative peace that twenty first century Northern Ireland is currently enjoying, there is more room for the prophetic now that the pastors can bring God's comfort into the greater normalcy of life.

The ongoing struggle to overcome sectarianism is an essential task for Ireland's Christians. The Christendom mindset whereby religious definition implies political definition is disappearing. In a new Ireland such tribal identification cannot be tolerated any longer. Part of the price of peace is for Christian denominations to confess their role in maintaining the conflict, at the same time as others acknowledge the Church's role in enabling and facilitating the path to peace. It is part of the Church's mission to finally withdraw from sectarianism and an essential task in order to make a missional impact in the future. The failure of Protestant denominations to make any real evangelistic impact among nominal Catholics in Northern Ireland, and vice versa, is a stark warning of the future failure of Christianity in an Ireland that is moving, slowly, from sectarianism. Any argument that the Church can be missional in the divided communities in Northern Ireland by keeping a sectarian profile and so relate to particular communities, falls far short of the calling of God's people.

Doing theology

Ireland has produced numerous internationally recognised poets and authors, but fewer eminent theologians. C S Lewis, and recently Alister McGrath and Chris Wright, are notable but their third level educations and subsequent careers have been beyond Ireland and consequently they have made little direct contribution to contextual missional thinking. Those who work beyond Ireland also include David Ford and Alan Ford who, after initial third level education in Ireland, have both made significant contributions teaching theology in Cambridge and Nottingham respectively. Billy Abraham, after his move to USA, has become an important theological voice for world Methodism. Presbyterian theologians have included Ernest Davey, J L M Haire and John Thompson while a list of significant recent Roman Catholic theologians includes Dermot Lane, Donal Dorr, Michael Hurley, Cahal Daly, Brendan Leahy, James McEvoy, Enda McDonagh and Vincent Twomey. Yet arguably there has been no recent Irish theologian who has risen to international prominence through reflection based primarily in Ireland. Despite the depth of Irish Christianity and the scholarly emphasises of St Patrick's College, Maynooth and Union Theological College, among others, Irish Christianity is not producing much significant Christian thought.

What is needed is sustained contextual reflection on mission in Ireland. This needs to be reconsidered regularly. Formerly a generation, about every thirty years, was thought to be enough but today, such is the pace of change, that contextual reflection has a shelf life of perhaps as little as five years. In particular, such contextual theology and missiology is lacking from the Protestant community. This gap needs to be addressed in order for more meaningful mission to happen in Ireland. The traditional ways of thinking and doing are no longer adequate to meet the postmodern challenge of contemporary Ireland. Imaginative reflection is necessary in order to give an authentic Christian response. Without this critical engagement there will either be a repetition of the failing practices of today (often models of mission uncritically imported from elsewhere) or else a shallow understanding leading to weak and limited practice. Irish society will increasingly ignore a superficial Christianity.

Sustained theological reflection is needed to engage with these issues.

Changing Theology – There is a tendency to seek to reinterpret theological understandings when society undergoes changes. This was part of the background to Vatican II and to the 'Honest to God' debate within British Protestantism in the 1960s, holding the view that the world is changing and so doctrine needs to change to keep pace. Yet this is ignoring that Christianity is the faith delivered once and for all to God's people. It is not a set of philosophical concepts that can be continually reinterpreted. Christian doctrine is either true or it is not.

Does Irish theology need to change? I can see no justification for changing what is fundamental to the gospel. The historic creeds are no more in need of overhaul in the twenty first century than in any previous century. Their content is solid, even if its expression needs continual renewal. But not all that is the faith of Irish Christians is based on scripture and the creeds. Much is tradition and interpretation. Consequently there are elements of the Irish faith that are negotiable in the current generation (clerical celibacy within Catholicism for one) but what does need fundamental attention is the expression of the faith. Irish Christianity needs to be expressed in ways that make sense to those who are still listening. The tragedy is that many have stopped listening, and for some who are still trying the message is just unintelligible. A clear, relevant, contextual presentation and demonstration of the gospel still makes an impact. Too often what is presented is neither clear nor relevant, and what is demonstrated is a further step removed.

The substance of Irish Christianity is sound. It is the gospel that has stood the test of time for two thousand years. The gospel does not need to be rewritten to appeal to the contemporary Irish. But it does need represented and re-interpreted.

Lay Theology - There has been a recent revival in theological study. Increasing numbers are studying theology at university level. Formerly most third level theological education was confined to the seminary but today more lay people than trainee clergy are studying theology. The discipline has been rescued from the seminary and now is the possession of laity. Theological reflection by clergy, even when employed as full time academics, generally has an ecclesial bias no matter how aware the writer is of this issue. Lay theology has the possibility, although by no means the certainty, to escape from this preoccupation. Lay theology is additionally more likely to be by women, voices not traditionally heard in Ireland. Of course, almost all theological reflection in Ireland has been lay reflection. All believers are theologians and what is happening today is the fulfilment of the desire for believers to be able to reflect on and articulate their faith understanding.

Theological reflection is changing in Ireland and while the future will be very different to the past, the future is looking hopeful. If Christianity is to become a movement rather than an institution, then theological reflection will have to be wrestled from the control of clergy as custodians of the institution. Unconsciously this is happening and is a further sign of the development of Christianity as a movement.

Education

Schools, with traditionally a Protestant or Catholic ethos, were places of denominational instruction under Christendom. Recent moves to develop integrated schools in the north and non-denominational Gaelscoileanna in both north and south challenge this. The Catholic Church has not been encouraging to the integrated school movement, some elements perceiving it as an attempt by culturally Catholic parents to remove their children from Catholic education without needing to enrol them in a state or virtual Protestant school. In the past it has been difficult for some Catholic parents of children in the integrated school sector to have their children confirmed and receive first communion. What needs to be recognised by Catholic authorities is the reality of the situation and that the integrated education sector is a positive missional opportunity. Chaplains should be appointed where invited and families, whose decision for integrated education points to a possible disillusionment with at least aspects of Irish Catholicism, should be actively encouraged to participate in the Church initiation rites without difficulties being raised. Under Christendom such would have been considered as straying families who needed discipline and punishment. Post-Christendom these are families who, in many cases, have already gone and so need to be wooed and won back. Attractive programmes and enthusiastic welcomes are the order of the day, rather than second-class treatment. That the returning prodigal appears to get a better welcome than the non-straying son is part of the gospel story.

The Gaelscoileanna sector is an appeal to an Irish identity that can appear to bypass the Catholic component that used to be essential in the Irish DNA. With a long pedigree, the last fifteen years have witnessed a rapid growth of such schools and today there are around two hundred found across the whole of Ireland. An initial education through the Irish medium at a gaelscoil is an increasingly attractive option to many. It has been criticised as an 'indulgence' of the wealthy with fee paying schools achieving a form of social segregation but that claim is without much substance, particularly in the Republic of Ireland where there is traditionally a major fee paying sector at post primary level. In Northern Ireland the Gaelscoileanna is not just a nationalist alternative to the state sector. Integrated education largely achieves this without the need to learn through Irish. Rather, there is a part of this movement that is a post Catholic expression that seeks to identify with an Irish heritage without the need to go through Catholicism to achieve this. An interesting development will be whether a significant number of non Irish background children begin to be educated in these schools. There is also a Catholic Church involvement in this sector that needs to be increased. This is not to wrest control of the education of part of the population back into institutional hands. Rather it is a missional opportunity towards a group that has chosen to go beyond the bounds of Church control.

In Northern Ireland the Protestant school, or more accurately state school that happened to have an overwhelming nominally

Protestant enrolment and often Protestant Church representatives on Boards of Governors, was a place of Protestant denominational teaching. As a child I sat in a class that for one hour a week was separated into Anglicans, Presbyterians and others. As an 'other' it was usually the Methodist minister who took this group but the three clergy came to teach their denominational understanding of Christianity to primary age children. That has largely gone. There is a small 'Christian School' movement, based on similar movements in the USA. The Free Presbyterian Church has established a small number of schools run along the lines of their understanding of Christianity but this appears to be remaining a very fringe movement and is not a model as to how churches should missionally engage in this area.

Part of the answer is to recognise the advantage of secular education. Under Christendom education was Christian education and, frankly, in Ireland too many mistakes were made. The place for Christian education is primarily in the home of Christian parents and secondly in the local worshipping congregation. The school should be religiously neutral although religion should still feature in the curriculum in a significant way to reflect its importance in the past, present and future of Ireland. Christians should not need or desire the state school to promote Christianity but nor should a school promote secularism or any other ideology. The growth in numbers taking Christianity or religion as a subject at GCSE or Junior Certificate is an example of increasing interest. Christians do not need to defend the teaching of religion as a subject in school. That is not under threat. It is the narrow denominational teaching in the state system that needs to be repudiated. If not, then it is equally appropriate for a Muslim teacher to use the opportunity of classes in religion to promote a particular Islamic perspective.

When the local congregation recognises that it is Christian parents and the church community who have the responsibility for passing on an understanding of Christian faith, and the faith itself, then a missional mindset towards children and young people becomes necessary. All activities to engage with young people become, of necessity, missional. Youth clubs are increasingly disappearing from local congregations. Part of the

114

reason for this is positive in that they arose when there was little recreational provision for young people and youth clubs were a Church response to this issue. Today increasing affluence, increasing expectation and a level of state provision makes the sort of contribution that most local churches can make in this area largely redundant. Congregations should recognise this not as failure but as part of the development of society. The day of the local church youth club has largely gone although rural areas still have a need for this type of activity as local councils cannot provide such facilities on a comprehensive scale. Today a more overtly missional engagement is needed. This is being seen in numerous places where imaginative schemes are being undertaken, such as in Blackrock where a Methodist church building was turned into a 'night club' type of youth centre and a resident team engaged with local young people in a wide variety of programmes. The danger is if this is seen by the Church as a contemporary, expensive rebirth of the youth club. It needs always to be missional; to have the motivation of introducing young people to the Christian faith. This no longer happens at school and the decline in Christian belief and observance means it is very unlikely to happen in the average Irish home. The local church needs both to be and to be perceived of as a place where Christianity is clear and obvious. The good news of Jesus cannot be a two minute slot fitted in before closing time. It needs to permeate and drive every part of the venture.

The traditional Protestant Sunday School is increasingly hard to maintain. The idea that children would meet for an hour before morning service for a school like experience of Christianity gradually developed into a forty minute escape from the main service where more age appropriate activities sought to convey the central tenets of Christianity. This is now starting to collapse. Many smaller congregations no longer have a sufficient critical mass around which to base age related activities. Even among families that attend church there is increased pressure from sporting, musical, educational and other cultural events happening on Sundays. Fewer people are able to commit the time needed to teach Sunday School type classes. In many congregations the work that volunteers previously did is now carried out by a paid youth or children's worker. Church members will increasingly commit their money but not their time to such work. The vitally important child protection legislation and resultant police checks make the recruitment of 'casual' leaders for such groups more problematic and it all points to an impending crisis for this traditional way of sharing faith with a younger generation.

Of increasing popularity in recent years has been the use of 'Holiday Clubs'. Thematic material is produced by a number of organisations detailing all that is necessary for a local church to run a very attractive, high energy holiday programme for children. These are very effective in the Easter and summer holidays and many parents, who have little church involvement, are still happy to have their children attend these normally very well run events, even if they primarily view such events as a 'cheap and cheerful' way of entertaining and minding their children. Congregations can learn from this as an effective form of mission. It engages with a generation that has become detached from Christianity and presents Christian faith in an attractive manner – such is the stuff of good mission. Rather than putting increasing energy into failing Sunday Schools, congregations can re-orientate themselves to a more inclusive Sunday worship that does not separate children from parents and focus on Christmas, Easter and summer holiday periods as times of enhanced mission to this younger generation. Catholic congregations, with a drift towards some of these activities, have a lot to learn from this Protestant experience to avoid discovering a model that might be relatively new to them but is already virtually redundant.

An interesting variation is to run such a 'Holiday Club' for elderly people. A few local congregations have recently tried this in England. A local church might be in an area with a predominately elderly population. During the traditional English holiday month of August most community activities cease and often the extended families of these elderly people will be away on holiday. The month can be long and dull for elderly people and so some congregations, from a missional perspective, have started to put on specific activities for elderly during August.

Sport

If Christianity has been declining as the faith of Ireland, sport has been increasing. The GAA has always had a fervent following and been inextricably linked to Catholicism. In Northern Ireland the soccer teams tend to have tribal support bases, even if the players now come from a more diverse background. The arrival of the first foreign professionals into Irish soccer helped to break the sectarian hold on team selection. A North African Muslim player for Linfield did not fit easily into the denominational distinctiveness of the local tribal divisions which started to crack, if not fully crumble, in the 1980s.

The virtual identification of sport as religion in Ireland came through the unlikely person of England's Jack Charlton. With a messiah-like quality he resurrected the Republic of Ireland's soccer team to world parity and a World Cup quarter-final appearance in Italy in 1990. That this competition also included a visit for the team to Pope John Paul II only cemented the sporting and religious mixture. In the pre-Celtic Tiger and pre ceasefire era this was a singular success story for Ireland and foreshadowed much that was to follow. The passion and fanaticism exhibited by sports fans and players are easily compared to religious devotion but significant missional opportunities are available through sport.

Chaplains - The position of chaplains within sporting organisations is a fairly recent development and while it does have Christendom overtones it is a helpful missional approach that can be replicated elsewhere. Representative Christians are involved as chaplains in the life of the sporting club to offer pastoral support, if not divine intervention, and are able to relate on many levels to players and staff. Most of those associated with such clubs, especially if they are urban based, no longer have an active connection with a Christian community, even if a tribal identification is obvious. This chaplaincy takes the Christian hope beyond the confines of the faith community and engages with those on the outside. It is largely pastoral support, sharing in the individual's highs and lows as well as those of the team.

Such chaplaincy exhibits the humility of contemporary mission in that it exists by invitation of the club and the opening normally comes through the cultivation of friendships and the sense that the club has something to benefit from the relationship.

Sporting icons – The days of Maynooth Seminary having a handful of county players at any given time is long gone. But there is a major missional and evangelistic role for the cultural icon that is the contemporary sporting hero. In an era when young people (and others) are unwilling to listen to the voice of parents, teachers, clergy, politicians and others who used to influence communities, the voice of the sporting or music star is avidly consumed. The portrayal of Christianity as an attractive and relevant lifestyle is effectively carried out through such 'role models'. Americans are used to many of their sporting heroes acknowledging the place of faith in their success. Not so the recent Irish. A rugby player such as Andrew Trimble, who regularly shares about the impact his Christian faith has on his life and career, is the sort of individual who can potentially influence a generation that has become disillusioned with much else.

John 3:16 – Sporting events in Ireland regularly draw the largest physical attendance and TV audience. One evangelistic tactic in recent years has been for a couple of Christians to sit behind the posts at a soccer or Gaelic football match and when a goal or point is scored they lift their banner which might read 'John 3:16' or something equally enigmatic. The idea is that the armchair fan, who watches the goal being replayed a dozen times, keeps noticing the banner. If they are unaware just what 'John 3:16' is about, it becomes a conversation point in the pub or home. Eventually somebody suggests it might be a verse from the Bible and a discussion continues. Such an approach is missionally effective in contemporary Ireland as it is subtle, provokes a question rather than confronts with an answer, occurs far from the confines of a church building and participates in the joys and sorrows of a local community as it is mirrors the fortunes of the local team.

Identity

In the Republic of Ireland the first years of the twenty-first century witnessed something that seemed, for the previous eighty years, to be impossible – significant growth in the traditional Protestant denominations. Census figures, and other indicators, have confirmed the visible growth and revitalisation of many of these formerly declining congregations. Christians from Africa and Asia, often the fruit of Irish missionary endeavour, have come to Ireland and bolstered congregations across the country. The picture is patchy and Methodism and Presbyterianism in particular have been positively impacted but it has brought a new missional opportunity for the traditional Protestant community in the Republic of Ireland related to identity.

The 'Others' - For generations Irish Protestants were Protestants before they were Irish, that is if they were considered Irish by the wider community or even perceived themselves as Irish. Despite all the history of Protestant involvement in and at times leadership of the early nationalist movement, to be authentically Irish in the twentieth century was to be Catholic. Protestants, with their establishment ethos and plantation background, were 'the other'. Today this is increaseingly no longer the case. Due to the growth of Muslim, Hindu and Buddhist communities, Irish Protestants are now perceived as Irish in a way these recent newcomers are not, or at least not yet. Protestants may still be a bit strange, but through shared history, shared English language (ironically) and the more obviously common features of Christianity they are much more recognisable than the new 'others' in Irish society. Missionally Protestants have never had it so good. In an era of reducing Catholic dominance, of cultural icons coming from the Protestant community, and the ending of the horrors of Protestant violence in the north, Protestants have now been finally accepted as Irish.

The days of 'souperism' are gone and, with the exception of a few areas in the South West of Ireland, this legacy is disappearing. When Protestants articulate their faith in the public arena it is more often seen as an interesting alternative to the perceived 'old fashioned' voice of Catholicism. Catholics look with interest as to how married clergy fulfil their ministry, rather than askance as in a previous generation. Protestant schools are increasingly attractive to Catholic parents and the days when Catholics avoided Trinity College, Dublin are in the distant past. The arrival of those who are perceived as more distinctly different has helped create a more neutral arena for Protestants to share their understanding of faith. Protestants can engage missionally in contemporary Ireland in a way unknown to their forebears.

The crude fact that there are now more Protestants in the Republic of Ireland than for a couple of generations means that the capacity for mission is greatly increased. The maintenance mentality that characterised much Protestant work in the Republic of Ireland over the last eighty years needs to be replaced with a confident, missional orientation. The days of seeing simple survival as 'success' are long gone and the missional opportunities of today's Ireland need to be grasped. This is starting to happen but needs to be a more conscious orientation. A new mindset or paradigm shift is needed.

The skills that assisted a ministry focusing on maintenance are not the same skills that are needed for mission. It might be that a completely new order of 'Pioneer Ministry' is needed. This has recently been initiated in the Church of England, recognising that in a post-Christendom context a new form of ministry is needed. It might be that ordained ministry itself needs to be challenged as a way of enabling mission. If, as has been argued earlier, mission is primarily undertaken by lay people, the training or retraining of clergy becomes largely an irrelevancy with regard to mission. The equipping of the congregation to missional engage is the priority.

Ireland is witnessing a reassessment of how many of its denominations train clergy. Catholic seminaries have been closed with St Patrick's College, Maynooth now the main focus of preparation. Methodists and Anglicans are revamping their ministerial training with a broader focus on what ministry means. Presbyterians, with more robust numbers training for ministry, have not embarked on the depth of soul searching of some of the others. The smaller Protestant denominations have usually had a flexible approach to ministerial preparation, and some strands have never had ordained clergy. Yet there is not a debate about the importance of equipping the people of God as the priority. In an institution it is the guardians and employees of the institution who primarily influence any change of direction. Institutional change is often slow. In a movement, where much more rapid change is both possible and necessary, the focus is on all rather than just a few. Until Irish Christianity is willing to shed its institutional layers it will fail to adequately address the need to see its training for mission as a training of the whole people of God primarily and allocate its resources accordingly. This is a missionally imperative issue. Anything less is tinkering with a system that has largely broken down.

Catholic Protestants

Until recently, if you were Catholic and wanted to express your faith in a different way, your choice was a Protestant denomination or nothing. This involved a surrender of cultural identity as much as religious orientation. Traditionally there are not many Celtic shirts in a Protestant congregation. The last twenty years have witnessed the creation of a network of new congregations in the Republic of Ireland comprised of people from a Catholic background who want to express their faith in a way that is similar to some of the Protestant denominations but does not have the cultural baggage associated with them.

The missional implications are obvious. No longer is it necessary to reject cultural Catholicism in order to express Christianity in a way other than mainstream Catholicism. A renewed Christian faith can be accommodated within a familiar cultural identity. This form of Christian expression is not found in Northern Ireland. It may be that the cultural ambiguities that are involved in a Protestant style of Christianity within a socially Catholic milieu are just too nuanced for the more clear-cut life expressed north of the border.

Is this a sign of reformed Catholicism or Catholic Protestantism? Probably neither. It is more likely a rejection of both Catholicism and Protestantism as expressed in Ireland.

Because Protestantism historically failed to become the faith of Ireland and remained the preserve of the descendants of planters and garrisons it is not viewed as a suitable faith destination for the majority. Dissident Catholic movements have not been able to maintain the title of Catholic. Whether it is a conservative holding to the Tridentine mass in the tradition of Archbishop Lefebvre or a more liberal interpretation of Catholicism as exemplified by 'Bishop' Pat Buckley, such movements are outside of what it means to be Roman Catholic. Above all, Roman Catholicism involves appropriate allegiance to the Vatican authorities. Catholics who want to express their faith in a way that owes more theological loyalty to varieties of Protestantism can still be culturally Catholic but that is all.

One Protestant denomination that surprisingly has bucked this trend is the Baptist Church in the Republic of Ireland. Its historic background and introduction to Ireland is as the faith expression of Cromwell's chaplains and a number of current congregations trace their roots back to that era. However, due to its historically small numbers in the Republic of Ireland, it was not associated with the three 'mainstream' Protestant denominations (Anglican, Presbyterian and Methodist). In recent years there has been a significant growth within a number of Baptist congregations and the planting of new congregations. Many of these new members are from a Catholic background and have seen the abandonment of their Catholic cultural identity as a price worth paying. The important factor seems to be that while they were leaving behind their traditional cultural expression, they were not associating with one of the obviously 'British' expressions. The independency of each Baptist congregation allows a local and consequently Irish perspective to develop in a way that the more denominationally minded Anglicans, Presbyterians and Methodists have found very difficult. The Baptists seem to occupy a space somewhere between Irish Catholicism and British Protestantism, despite the staunchly Plantation and English roots of the denomination. Missionally it shows other Protestants in the Republic of Ireland that an historic link to a British identity is not an insurmountable problem but illustrates the importance of an indigenous leadership and local autonomy as missional factors.

The Evangelical Alliance Ireland is the bridge between these new congregations and traditional Protestantism. Not all historic Protestants are willing to join with this grouping, viewing it as a more evangelistic form of faith than they are comfortable with. The missional aspect of this is that through this new group the passion and enthusiasm for mission that the new congregations are bringing is rubbing off on some of the older and long established Protestant congregations.

How does Catholicism respond to this? With a Christendom mindset the institution would seek to dominate, control and defeat this new threat. However, with the outlook of a movement, Catholicism can see this as a pointer to renewal. This movement is not a threat to Catholicism. Rather it is an example of cultural Catholics wanting a different style of faith expression without wishing to abandon their Catholic DNA. Catholicism needs to learn from this vibrancy of faith, lay leadership and stress on scripture over tradition. It does not mean that Catholicism as a whole is to change to replicate these new congregations, but it does show one of the ways in which Catholicism needs to develop.

Secularism

The pivotal year was 1973, when violence in the north was coming to a peak and both the UK and Republic of Ireland joined the European Union (a year that also marked the final retirement of Eamon de Valera as President, the death of Archbishop McQuaid and the election of the Protestant Erskine Childers as de Valera's successor). This turned out to be hugely significant as the European influence on Ireland helped lead to economic regeneration and social liberalism and the eventual secularism that has developed more recently. Such secularism can be understood as good news for mission in Ireland.

Secularism removes the role of institutional Christianity from a dominant place in the nation. The traditional secularisation theory understood that religion would slowly wither and die, society was coming of age and a mature society would outgrow the need for religious legitimation. That clearly has not happened in Ireland and most elsewhere. A quick glance at contemporary Russia shows that after seventy five years of communism and aggressive secularisation the Church did not disappear but continued to re-emerge post Communism and quickly regain a surprising measure of influence. The Russian Orthodox Church is an example of an institution being reborn and attempting to rebuild a form of Christendom with the consequent disapproval of any alternative forms of faith. More recently a revised secularisation theory argues for the decline of Christendom and the public role of faith institutions but that the outcome is a privatisation of faith rather than its disappearance.

This seems to equate more closely with what is happening and is good news for the movement called Christianity that is being reborn in Ireland. A movement is primarily concerned with influencing individuals. It does not ignore the societal dimension but that will be achieved primarily through the collective actions of faithful individuals rather than through the Christendom approach. The perception of faith as primarily an individual concern rather than a community issue allows the missional approach of a movement to be potentially effective.

Secularisation limits the impact of Christian institutions. In Ireland these institutions are in rapid decline and my argument is that this is largely good news as it allows a movement to emerge. Ireland is not yet a secular nation but this trend towards a privatised faith encourages Irish Christians to abandon the struggle to maintain the weakening institutions of Christendom. It is international trends rather than just Irish factors that are causing this weakening. Ireland is not witnessing the death of Christianity but sharing with Europe and beyond a form of secularisation that sees the retreat of institutional Christianity from the public square but also witnesses the increasing importance of faith issues in a more spiritual and multi-faith society.

Mission to Catholicism or Catholic Mission?

Base Christian Communities (BCC) have never been influential in Ireland in the way that this movement impacted South American Catholicism from the 1960s onwards. There have been small experimental communities, often located in inner cities or on deprived housing estates, usually led by secular or religious clergy and resulting from a decision by those from the outside to attempt to impact a community. A reconsideration of this approach is timely as its day may finally have come in Ireland. A BCC has among its characteristics a stress on lay leadership, incarnational living, a relational approach and a rereading of scripture with fresh eyes. As such it reflects a movement more than an institution. The South American BCC should be viewed as a model rather than a blueprint and brings the strong missional understanding that mission is primarily what Christians are before anything that they do. Such communities potentially overcome the disjunction between belief and practice that has bedevilled Irish Christianity in the last generation. To be missionally effective a BCC needs an authentically Irish voice and appearance that cannot be imposed from outside but it does offer an approach that has had missional impact elsewhere. Missionally BCCs resonate with Ireland's current Catholic context as they are low cost in terms of finance and clergy, focus on authenticity and local relationships, and stress personal faith and evangelisation. In the 1960s a BCC in Ireland was an interesting ecclesial experiment. Today it may be a missional essential.

The most effective mission field for this approach may well be lapsed Catholics. This numerous community has not necessarily rejected Catholicism but has at least drifted away from any meaningful connection. The BCC approach offers a renewed form of Catholicism that shares some of the features of the Protestant movement but is still very obviously Catholic. It is connected to the parish structure but not limited to this rather medieval way of determining church association.

While the BCC offers significant missional possibilities caution is required. Since its development in South America in the 1960s, that formerly most Catholic of continents has been rapidly turning Protestant, or more accurately Pentecostal. The Pentecostal community in this region is now measured in the hundreds of millions, the first generation of these coming from at least a nominal Catholic background. The BCC did not renew Catholicism in South America. Yet this factor may well be the pointer to why it is so needed in contemporary Ireland. The 'failure' of the BCC in South America was entwined with a struggle with institutional Catholicism. Ironically this struggle was largely won by the 1990s with the mainstream acceptance of the BCCs but by that time millions of Catholics had already left for Pentecostal groups that stressed lay participation, the reading of scripture and personal relationships – all BCC emphasises. A BCC approach, Catholic in ethos but largely independent from the institution, may well be missionally much more effective.

Renewed Catholicism

The most effective missional approach and missional community for the Republic of Ireland is a renewed Catholicism. Other forms of Christianity are making an impact but in numerical terms this is small and the indications are that while the Protestant communities are likely to continue to grow, this will be incremental rather than making a large impact. This has been the history of post reformation Ireland and it is unlikely to be different in the future. Within parts of mainstream Irish Protestantism, with awareness that Christianity is far broader than each denominational perspective, and with a missional desire to impact Ireland, there is increasing awareness that the most effective thing they can do is seek to influence the renewal of Catholicism with the resultant missional impact this will make.

Renewal comes at a risk, as has already been alluded to with reference to contemporary Russia and the rebuilding of Christendom. The danger of Catholicism seeking renewal is that there is the temptation to seek to rebuild a form of Christendom. Renewal can be viewed as a way to repair what is acknowledged as broken and restore the former glory, influence and position of the Church in society. It needs to be understood as a process of change. A renewed Catholicism will be different to both present and former Catholicism. So, where is Catholicism in need of renewal to enable such a renewed community to make a missional impact in Ireland?

Voices – Irish Catholicism needs to listen more than speak. Like most, Catholicism has been quick to issue statements and

126

pronouncements but not so quick to consult. Various forums have been attempted to give voice to lay people and in particular women but none have proved particularly effective. There needs to be a collective will to find an efficient way of hearing the concerns of all church members. Rather than a controlling mechanism or a safety valve to allow views to be expressed and somehow feel that this expression is achieving something, such a forum needs to impact Catholicism and be part of the necessary change and development.

The voices of ordinary clergy need also to be heard. In an institutional hierarchy there is an ascending order of loudness by the participants. Ordinary clergy often understand more clearly the needs and aspirations of lay members than the hierarchy who spend so much more of their time in the company of other clergy.

Hierarchy – Irish Catholicism has a diocesan structure based on historic boundaries that bear little relation to contemporary population concentrations. Part of the consequence of this is that there are more dioceses and bishops than is needed, especially so if a renewed Catholicism is more akin to a movement than an institution. Dioceses should be merged, perhaps on the retirement of current office holders, and a simpler Catholicism slowly developed.

Additionally, the role of these local bishops needs to significantly change. Under John Paul II's leadership there was a strengthening of the role of the Vatican and its curia and at times bishops appeared to be viewed as little more than branch officials whose only function was to act on behalf of the parent organisation. Almost any issue that did not have a clearly prescribed answer needed to be referred back to the HQ. A consequence of this centralisation is that Catholicism has become more of an international brand than a local expression. It is important that local bishops lead. This is not an attack on Vatican influence, but a reassertion of the local expression of Christianity.

Enculturation is an important missional consideration. The foreign missionaries, especially since the 1950s, put great efforts into enabling a form of Christianity that made sense in the particular local context as experience had shown that contextual Christianity was more missionally effective. Christendom did not need or value such individual responses, indeed it sought to bring uniformity. Catholicism is in danger of remaining caught in this Christendom and globalising mindset. Today it is not a missional advantage that Catholicism appears much the same in Cork, Calcutta and Caracas. The McDonaldisation of Catholicism is a problem not an advantage.

Archbishop Dairmuid Martin may have a pivotal role. He occupies an interesting position as one who is perceived as being progressive and who has recognised the weakness of the authoritarian approach that Irish Catholicism has so often exhibited, surely the ideal person to oversee renewal. But there is one inherent danger to this. Martin spent twenty-seven years as a senior and highly regarded Vatican official. Such a background tends to give a disproportional place to the role of the Vatican and the institution and among the challenges facing Martin is to consider loosening the hold of the institution he served so successfully over the one he currently serves.

Vatican II – A renewed Catholicism needs to be based on the teachings of Vatican II, or at least until there is a Vatican III. Irish Catholicism proved itself a relatively loyal son in implementing the legislation that flowed from the congress such as liturgy in the vernacular, the priest facing the people, relaxation of the ban on meat on Fridays and so on. The letter of the law was followed. What Irish Catholicism proved less enthusiastic about was in implementing the spirit of the law. The process begun at Vatican II contains enough energy and insight to continue to bring renewal if its ethos is eagerly embraced. A reluctant acquiescence to change does not bring renewal.

In its refusal to fully embrace the spirit of Vatican II Irish Catholicism showed itself to be out of the mainstream of Catholic practice and this has a missional consequence. Without any dramatic departure from wider Catholicism a renewed Irish Catholicism can result from a closer adherence to the heart of contemporary Catholic expression. Lapsed Catholics are often lapsed because of some perceived deficiencies with the Church. These people have not associated, at least in significant numbers, with any other faith expression and retain much of the cultural trappings of Catholicism. A renewed Catholicism brings a call to return to a changed Church. Whether there will be any widespread return is uncertain, but return is the likely direction if there is to be any movement.

Evangelisation

Alongside cultural Catholicism 'á la carte Catholicism' needs to be added. Under Christendom it was necessary to accept or adhere to the whole system. Postmodernity brings a variety of responses, one of which is to retain a Catholic identity but choose what to accept or reject. For example, rejection of the Church's teaching on birth control used to put an individual outside of the fold. Today you can still be basically a good Catholic but have abandoned that part of Church teaching. The good news for mission is that today people are more likely to be open to Christianity as a spiritual identity when they perceive that it does not immediately require control over all areas of their life. Does this compartmentalisation of faith equate to a living and saving relationship with Jesus Christ? Possibly not, but what it does allow is an initial experience of Jesus Christ that gives opportunity for a more complete relationship to develop.

Celtic Mission

Despite their recent decline there is increasingly a renewed place for convents and monasteries in contemporary Ireland. Under Christendom the parish was the main focus and evangelism was more a policing of the beliefs and morals of the community within this geographical area. The Roman victory at the Synod of Whitby in 664 led to the marginalisation of the monastery that had been the main means of evangelisation in Celtic Ireland. The collapse of Christendom is not necessarily the collapse of the parish system (although the current national system staffed by clergy is unsustainable) but there is a renewed place for monastic communities in evangelisation.

Monasteries and convents, post Vatican II, increasingly opened themselves to the community and many became involved in leading retreats and mission programmes. It is among the members of these orders that are found many of Ireland's most articulate Christian communicators. But the main missional advantage is the neutrality of the monastery as against the parish where the community gather. With the privatisation of faith such neutral spaces are increasingly important.

Monasteries and convents are also private in the sense that it is individuals by choice who come rather than the local community at prayer. There is an anonymity in participating in programmes in such places that is not found elsewhere. Of course, the city centre and even large town centre parish church is taking on this level of anonymity due to the dispersal of the community and the lack of social interaction between those who are geographically close but not close in any other indicator of community. As network rather than geography starts to dominate social interaction, there is an implication − not necessarily negative- for the local church to grapple with. This should not be decried as the end of community. Rather it is part of the ongoing evolution of community. Anonymity has positive missional implications as a person's faith search and faith journey need not be public knowledge. There is greater incentive to cross boundaries and do something new when not under public scrutiny. Someone from a Protestant background may well feel more comfortable participating in an event in a monastery than in a local Catholic parish church. It is no coincidence that the decline in levels of individual morality in Ireland occurred as society was becoming increasingly privatised. Beyond the 'Big Brother' (or more likely 'Big Mother') eye of Irish society, new forms of behaviour took root. The same can be true for spiritual practices.

What needs to happen is for these monasteries and convents to increasingly recognise the opportunities being presented to them and their evangelistic mandate. They need to become much more intentionally evangelistic communities with this task of evangelism alongside, and in many cases superseding, their existing charisms. These are the evangelistic centres of the present and future, engaging in mission on their own terms and equipping the people of God in their task of evangelisation.

Celtic Spirituality

A quick Google search for Celtic Spirituality reveals about 1.25 million sites. That there is great interest in all things Celtic is obvious, the success of Riverdance and the Celtic merchandising industry are testimony to that. Spirituality has also gained renewed interest as Chapter Three considered. However, Ireland is not resplendent with places to study Christian Celtic spirituality. Too much of this area has been abandoned to fringe Christian groups or avowed pagans.

Monasteries and convents are among the places well suited to engage in this area. An increasing number of courses and programmes, from the academic to the experiential, need to be provided. Even for many Irish Christians, disillusioned with the contemporary Church, there is a great resource to delve into where the Church was primarily an evangelistic movement. A recovery of the spirituality of the early Irish Christians and missionaries can only positively impact the present generation of believers. Those interested mainly in the Celtic or spirituality perspectives will encounter living, authentic Christianity when such programmes are run by believers. Increasing missional opportunities exist but the Church needs too be proactive and even entrepreneurial at times, in order to minister effectively in such a time as this.

With renewed confidence Irish Christians can engage in the doing of mission in contemporary Ireland. Part of the new background to this is the presence of sizeable numbers of people who follow many different religious faiths and these particular issues are considered in the next chapter.

Questions

1   What are your experiences of ecumenism? Can ecumenical mission work?

2   Are Irish people still sectarian, if a little more under the surface now?

3   How is mission as a movement different to mission as an institution?

Chapter Eight:
Mission and Inter-Faith Ireland

Does this subject justify a chapter in a book on mission in contemporary Ireland? If considered on the level of numbers of people of other faith in Ireland, then barely. However, given that this is an issue that has very rarely been considered within Ireland, despite the very extensive missionary engagement with people of other faiths outside Ireland, then the urgency of this reflection becomes clear. This is an initial consideration of the issues involved. Others need to reflect in this area. Chapter Two has given a brief overview of the Irish interaction with other faiths in Ireland and this whole area is dealt with in depth in *The Faiths of Ireland.* Christians in Ireland are only starting to take notice of the new religious reality of Ireland. This is the necessary first step before much missional thinking and activity develops. But that time has now come.

Irish Christians need the confidence to missionally engage with the newer Irish faith communities. That this has not yet happened much is a cause of regret and at least five main reasons for this inactivity can be isolated.

1 The significant increase in other faith communities has occurred at the same time as general Christian institutional decline in Ireland. When this is added to the immediate crisis caused by the abuse scandals, impacting more than just the Catholic Church, it is not hard to see that the missional implications of a few thousand Muslims arriving in Ireland has not been top of many Christian agendas. While not an excuse for the relative inaction, it is, to some extent, understandable.

2 There is a question of identity as Irish. The history of Irish Judaism shows a small level of historic interaction and then some inter-faith activity from the 1970s onwards and a decline as the Irish Jewish population declined. Statistics imply that the bulk of the Irish Jewish impact was between 1900 -2000 with the first couple of decades of the twenty first century probably witnessing the gentle disappearance of Irish Judaism primarily through migration. Ireland was a part of a journey for Jews, not a destination. With this precedent, Irish Christians overall have been very slow to engage with new populations, such as Muslims, as they are perceived as transient. Why make friends with your new neighbour if they are already thinking of moving on? However, all the indications from the Muslim community, through its early establishment of schools, religious and social institutions and engagement with wider society, is that the Muslim community views Ireland as a destination. The Muslim community is here to stay.

3   It may be that Irish Christianity has become captive to a form of political correctness that denies the sharing of faith due to the arrogance and presumptions of having a metanarrative that is somehow valid for all. The appropriateness of evangelism per se in a postmodern society has been discussed in Chapter Five. It is one thing to maintain in doctrine the appropriateness of evangelism, it is quite another thing to be authentically evangelistic. A recent lack of confidence in the validity of evangelism has hindered the encounter.

4   Most of the limited historic inter-faith encounter within Ireland operated with an ecumenical mindset. It was a twentieth century discovery by Irish Christians that their task was not to evangelise each other but recognise the faith in each other and work together. The Irish inter-faith organisations began in the 1970s at the height of the ecumenical movement in Ireland and followed a similar pattern by understanding Jews to be people of different but related faith. The Council for Christians and Jews still operates very like an ecumenical council, and the Northern Ireland Inter-Faith Forum and Dublin's Three Faiths Forum share these same characteristics. So Ireland's modest inter-faith engagement was mistakenly built on an ecumenical approach that is only valid for intra-Christian encounters. Inter-faith encounter is not the 'wider ecumenism' if it is understood as an extension of Christian ecumenism. How Christians relate to people of other faiths is very different to how they relate to other Christians.

5   Of greater issue is whether Irish Christianity has conceded a religious pluralism alongside the necessary political pluralism. Religious pluralism, the theological understanding

that there are many valid ways to God, should not totally take away the motivation for evangelism but does inevitably lead to a dilution of the desire to evangelise people of other faiths. The urgency has gone. Missional approaches are still possible but this theological perspective puts such encounters well down the list. There are many more urgent tasks calling for attention.

Mission and a Pluralist Society

Perhaps the dominant issue that has stunted much inter-faith missional encounter elsewhere is this question of pluralism. How does mission relate to religious pluralism? Pluralism, as a feature of society, is to be acknowledged and affirmed. Any other way is simply totalitarianism. Cultural pluralism is the acknowledgement that there are a number of alternative cultural perspectives that are valid. No one way should dominate. Of course Ireland, north and south, has not been particularly successful at accepting difference, nor was Christendom in any of its guises. Add Ireland to Christendom and it is no surprise that an affirmation of cultural pluralism has not been a constant in Ireland.

The missiological question is not the acceptance or otherwise of cultural pluralism. That is taken for granted as the norm in a developed, mature nation. The issue for mission is how Christians understand their relationship with people of other faiths.

The historic Christendom understanding was that Christianity was for the Christian nations, as defined by the religion of the ruler and seeking to convert individuals from other faith backgrounds did not fit in with this understanding. Indeed, this latter approach beyond the walls of Christendom ultimately challenged the homogeneity of Christendom itself. 'No salvation beyond the Church' was not an inter-faith understanding but a Christendom declaration that no deviant form of Christianity would be accepted by the dominant community. When the issue was actively considered, through the challenge of the missionary movement, there was normally an exclusive Christian perspective taken. In recent years a 'three position' paradigm came to dominate the discussion:

1. Christianity is exclusively the only way to God

2. Christianity includes those of sincere other faiths even if they are not aware of this

3. Christianity is one valid way to God among many other valid ways in a pluralist world

This paradigm has been rightly challenged in recent years as concentrating solely on the soteriological aspect of the discussion. This is an important aspect but not the only issue. Andrew Kirk, due to pejorative connotations of exclusivism and pluralism, has argued for a way of thinking that retains three categories but sees the possible range of understanding grouped under the headings of particularity (salvation is only available through the death of Christ and appropriated through faith and association with the Christian community), generality (salvation is through Christ but the means of appropriation are more widely available) and universality (where there are many ways of approaching God). Alister McGrath retains the three tradition categories but adds the possibility of an understanding of parallelism whereby the distinctive features of the various religions are maintained. Christian belief leads to a Christian conclusion in heaven, Buddhist belief to a Buddhist conclusion in Nirvana, Islamic faith to Paradise and so on. Any attempt to force all religious expressions to conform to one understanding of reality is problematic. Thus there are salvations rather than salvation.

A more helpful approach may be to have the soteriological question as part of the discussion but not the only issue. If the question is whether there is the possibility of a relationship with God in other faiths, then a more positive response is possible. If it is asked whether other faiths have some true knowledge of God in their theological formulations, once more a Biblical perspective would say yes. If the question of the possibility of God being at work, at least to some extent, in other faiths, once more it seems apparent that this is what the Bible teaches. A picture is built of God at work in a unique way through Christ and in particular in and through the Christian community, and related to this is God at work in other ways through many, but not necessarily all, religious traditions. The acceptance of the *missio Dei* leads to this conclusion. Thus there is uniqueness and inclusiveness within this relationship. Can we argue that God is at work in Ireland authentically through Christ and the Christian community, and is distinctively present in many other faith traditions and communities? Based on the above the answer is yes.

Within this positive assessment Christians still have a valid case for evangelisation of people of other faiths. The soteriological question cannot be ignored. Having a relationship with God or an awareness of God does not necessarily imply or involve a saving relationship. If Christianity is life in all its fullness (John 10:10) then the possibility of this form of life on earth needs to be offered to all, never mind the eternal consequences. It is not even necessary to judge other faiths as deficient regarding ultimate salvation to build a valid case for Christian evangelisation.

There is an equally valid case for allowing the same rights and freedoms for all missionary religions to evangelise. Freedom of religion needs to be just that. The freedom to share a particular religious belief is a basic human right and recognised as such in Article 18 of the United Nations Universal Declaration of Human Rights. That said, cults should not enjoy the same freedoms as part of the definition of a cult includes a demonstrably negative impact on individuals and society often disguised through hidden agenda and difficulty for those associated with the cult to leave easily.

There are a number of ways in which a missional engagement between Christians and people of other faiths needs to take place in Ireland today.

Partnership – There are numerous areas where the various faith communities can and should work together. People of faith are people of faith. The actual issues are of secondary importance. The main issue is whether there is the desire to work through the implications of being people of faith. In a society that ranges across religious indifference, spiritual inquiry, committed faith and religious fanaticism, people of faith have a lot in common with each other. The willingness for appropriate partnership is necessary. Given that various Christian leaders in

Northern Ireland have found it helpful to work on occasions with leaders from some paramilitary groups in order to enable the peace process, it should not be a major issue to accept the possibility of working with Muslims and/or Jews on mutually beneficial projects. It is more a case of just recognising this as a possibility.

Hospitality – This works on two levels. There needs to be a Christian willingness to offer hospitality. Recently arrived faith communities will benefit from a simple welcome in a community; this can extend to the offer of the use of premises for cultural or faith community activities. Christian congregations are not expected to offer the use of their worship centres for worship by other faith communities, but all short of that should be possible. However to think that Irish Christians simply need to offer is only part of the issue. Irish Christians need to learn to receive as well as give.

More recently established faith communities have been proactive in inviting their local community to share in cultural and festival celebrations. Often this works on the level of people being interested in the perceived exoticness of certain foods, music, liturgies etc and a level of paternalism can be involved. Here is an area where clergy, with their faith representative role, can be active in giving and accepting invitations, in participation where appropriate and responding with generosity. The participation of Christian clergy in the cultural events of these newer communities acts as an endorsement for others to become involved. But such participation needs to fall short of involvement in the religious worship of others. Christians are Christians not worshippers of some vague God to whom approaches can be made in various ways. Most other religious communities will not invite or expect Christians to participate in their religious liturgies but the lines between the cultural and religious dimensions of a faith community are often blurred. Care and discretion are needed to understand the appropriate level of involvement.

Integration – Northern Ireland knows all about religious ghettos and recent generations have strengthened rather than weakened the religious identity of individual communities. This problem does not need to be replicated. It is commonplace for religious communities to congregate in proximity to places of worship, especially if faith distinctive education is available. Dublin already has some areas where there is a significant Muslim population and has had areas where Jews traditionally lived. Whether Dublin's Jews built synagogues in areas where they were living, or whether they moved to areas where synagogues were built is a bit of a 'chicken and egg' scenario. While such concentration is probably inevitable, Ireland is advantaged by current integration of other faith populations throughout the island. Northern Ireland's too many uniform communities are not an example to emulate. A rainbow appearance demonstrating the variety of what it means to be Irish in the twenty first century can be the positive future. Such integration occurs when newcomers are welcomed, included and accepted. It needs to be active. If only passive, then the same mistakes from Northern Ireland and elsewhere will be repeated.

Education – Ireland has a history of denominational education. In previous generations to be of a different denomination to the majority made education at times very problematic with the only option being to experience life as a minority in a sometimes unhelpful institution. This has changed and today the experience of faith minorities in Irish schools is normally good, with general support for pupils wishing to follow the dietary, worship and clothing implications of their particular faith. This needs to be maintained and enhanced. Schools, many with a strong denominational emphasis, need to be places where faith is affirmed but also where proselytising or discrimination does not occur. This does not mean that religion has to be downplayed and schools become faith neutral environments. This is, to some extent, appropriate within the state sector, but is not necessary where a school has denominational sponsorship. Faith minorities need to be supported, affirmed and cherished, but also shown the faith perspective of the school they are attending. Issues regarding religious clothing or symbols, which are at variance with traditional school uniform, need to be tackled creatively. This is generally happening in Ireland, learning from the confrontation that different approaches currently bring in Britain and France. The Muslim head girl of an Irish Catholic school is not a contradiction, it is the future.

Evangelism – The case for the appropriateness of evangelism in a multi-faith context has already been made. This is what Irish Christianity has believed and acted out for most of its history beyond our shores. How can this be done in contemporary multi-faith Ireland? That sensitivity and honesty need to be paramount should not need reiterated. Carrying out activities, such as school enrolment, with a hidden evangelistic motive is not consistent with the gospel. Making the use of every opportunity, however, is most consistent. Irish Christians, at times, have felt that the verbal declaration of their understanding of Christianity constituted evangelism. Men in dark suits preaching in the open air to no-one in particular is a caricature, but like most caricatures is based on a degree of fact. Evangelism, to be worthy of the name, must mean the good news being communication in a way that can be understood.

Faith is communicated much more easily to a friend than to a stranger, to someone you know and who can readily see how your faith impacts your life. It is within the conversation of friends from different faith backgrounds that each naturally shares their beliefs and it is a place of mutual evangelism. The Christian is being evangelised as much as is evangelising. This is the way it is with friends – a mutual influencing. We listen to each other's music, participate in the important events of each other's life, share the joys and sorrows and understand how each thinks, acts and believes. This is a correct missional approach in postmodern Ireland.

Is it appropriate for a Christian community to develop an evangelistic strategy that 'targets' a particular faith community? I think the answer is yes, but great care needs taken not to abuse any position of power and to live by the golden rule of only doing to others what we are content to have done to us. Irish Christians have historically had missional approaches to Jewish communities beyond Ireland, notably through the Irish Presbyterian Church that developed a sensitive and holistic approach that sought to share the good news of Jesus while also involved in meeting social and other needs of Jewish communities in Germany and Syria. Within Ireland the Sisters of Zion have an apostolate to work among Ireland's Jewish community and raise awareness of the Jewish roots of Christianity. No evangelistic work should ever insult, abuse, threaten or frighten. Scripture is clear that when meeting those of other faiths a Christian response should never be aggressive (Luke 9:51-56). The same good principles of best practice apply to inter-faith evangelism, but provide the means by which such an evangelistic approach is still appropriate. Christianity is a missionary religion. Sharing faith with others is what Christians are called to do.

Dialogue

There is very little 'official' inter-faith dialogue in Ireland. Given the history of Northern Ireland where dialogue between parts of the fractured Christian community is problematic and politicians have held talks about talks about talks this is not so surprising but more needs to be done. Groups such as the Three Faiths Forum, the Northern Ireland Inter-Faith Forum and the two Councils for Christians and Jews provide an important function but need to be supplemented by so much more. But let us not fall into the mistake of failing to recognise the numerous ways that inter-faith dialogue can and does already take place in Ireland. In many ways, it is the denominations and leaders of the religious groups who are lagging behind their members in this (and other) area(s).

Under Christendom there was no need for dialogue. Who would you dialogue with? The only legitimate religious authority and faith was Christian. Anything else was condemned as deviant and subversive. There was simply no-one recognised as worthy of dialogue. As Ireland is only moving out of this era, albeit very rapidly, a dialogical mindset needs to be developed.

Types of Inter-faith Dialogue - There are a number of varieties of inter-faith dialogue.

141

1. Parliamentary style dialogue, stemming from the 1893 World's Parliament of Religions, part of the World's Fair in Chicago, is carried forward by the international interfaith organisations such as the Council for Christians and Jews, the International Association for Religious Freedom, the World Congress of Faiths, the Interfaith Alliance and the Temple of Understanding. Ireland has yet to experience this.

2. Institutional dialogue such as the regular meetings between representatives of the Vatican and The International Jewish Committee for Inter-religious Consultation. Again Ireland has yet to experience this to any significant level but now is the time for the various denominations to start to interact with the leadership of the more recently established faith communities.

3. Theological dialogue, which takes seriously the questions and challenges posed by people of other faiths, is now beginning. Discussions that formerly were just ecumenical are now starting to become inter-faith. Academic institutions such as the Irish School of Ecumenics and Trinity College, Dublin are leading the way in this.

4. Dialogue in community is where within local communities, perhaps a town or city, representatives of the various faith groups meet regularly to build relationships, plan shared events and discuss issues of mutual importance. Having some similarities to local ecumenical partnerships that now exist throughout Ireland, it is now time for such local groups to be initiated.

5. Dialogue of life is the search for good relationships in ordinary life. This is the form of dialogue most experienced in Ireland and is not to be underestimated. People interact in the workplace, school and neighbourhood and in the small everyday exchanges perceptions are changed, truths unconsciously communicated, faith is shared and life enhanced. It is mission as being. It is the ordinary followers of the faiths of Ireland who are doing this day by day. The leaders of the faiths of Ireland need to catch up.

6. Spiritual dialogue is the attempt to learn from other traditions of prayer and meditation. This happens when Irish

people, perhaps interested in meditation, start attending a Buddhist retreat centre and discover some of the riches of Buddhism and compare this to whatever Christian or other faith understanding they came with.

7. The dialogue of depth is where there is an ongoing commitment to the practice of dialogue within a community. This is the challenge before Ireland currently. To move beyond the first stages into a more sustained and committed dialogue where a journey is intentionally commenced with others.

8. The dialogue of faith is where people of faith meet together on an ongoing basis to discuss what their faith means to them and how this relates to the faith understanding of others.

Is Dialogue Biblical? - It is primarily in the ministry of Paul that a dialogical approach can be clearly discerned. When Paul ministered in the religiously diverse city of Ephesus he followed his normal pattern of going first to the Jews and there he was able to preach in the synagogue for three months (Acts 19:8). As usual Paul was on borrowed time and eventually opposition forced him to leave. Rather than move to another city Paul remained in Ephesus for a further two years, conducting his ministry by holding public lectures and discussions in the debating chamber of Tyrannus. The intriguingly named Tyrannus appears to have used the chamber for his own teaching in the morning, during which time Paul was financing his ministry by tent making (Acts 20:34). Paul was able to use the chamber during the hottest part of the day for his debates about faith issues. The interest these aroused was sufficient to continue for a couple of years, especially given that the discussions were conducted during the noon siesta period. When Paul was 'arguing persuasively' in the synagogue and lecture hall, the Greek root of the verb (*dialegomai*) tells us he was 'dialoguing', signifying at least a two-way conversation (Acts 19:8-10).

In Athens Paul, from what could be perceived as a position of weakness, engaged in dialogue with philosophers. As Paul was proclaiming the gospel he became involved in discussions with a few Epicurian and Stoic philosophers (Acts 17:16-34). Ridiculed and 'brought' to a public debate, Paul is invited to give his perspective on faith. The setting is where his listeners are comfortable and at home whilst Paul has stepped outside the familiar surroundings of the synagogue, house church, or even lecture hall where he set the agenda himself. In Athens there is an almost post-Christendom context. The Christian speaker is one voice among many, and a disadvantaged voice in that many find Paul's thoughts most bizarre. Within this context Paul's approach is to dialogue with the philosophers by using their religious concepts and thought forms. He is, in a sense, dialoguing himself between Christianity and Greek philosophical concepts and producing, not a synthesis but a Christianity that has come through a dialogical process in order to be communicable and relevant to his listeners.

When Jesus encounters a Samaritan woman he uses the dialogue of life to initiate an inter-faith conversation (John 4: 1-42). The features of this encounter are that it was most ordinary and natural, faith issues came up in the course of daily life, she talked to Jesus about her faith understanding, and Jesus' 'faith filled' conversation made a great impact on her and many of her friends and neighbours. Such is inter-faith dialogue.

When Elijah challenged the prophets of Baal was this an inter-faith dialogue (1 Kings 18:16-46)? I think the answer is no. The context was not the mutual meeting of people of different faiths but related to syncretistic developments within the people of Israel. Elijah was responding to a problem within the faith of Israel, a faith that was being corrupted, rather than objectively considering the merits of others worshipping Baal. Elijah did allow the prophets of Baal to speak and share something of their faith but it was more in the way of a power encounter, akin to St Patrick confronting the power of the Druids, than a mutual discussion. Two or more monologues do not make a dialogue. This story sits as a warning to Christians about the dangers of syncretism but does not invalidate a dialogical approach to mission.

Authentic Dialogue - For dialogue to be real there needs to be a mutual acceptance of each other. Christians can no longer claim dominance and a level playing field must be level for all. While this is a new place for Irish Christians to find themselves in, it is one that should be approached with confidence. In the mutual exchange of faith understandings the Christian needs to understand that, through the work of the Holy Spirit, Christ is active in the dialogue. He does not need protected or defended by us. Irish Christians can engage with confidence and enthusiasm.

In 1981 the following 'Four Principles of Inter Faith Dialogue' were agreed ecumenically by the British Council of Churches, based on the earlier World Council of Churches 'Guidelines on Dialogue with People of Living Faiths and Ideologies'. This still remains as best practice within the ecumenical movement and recognises that:

1. Dialogue begins when people meet each other

2. Dialogue depends upon mutual understanding and mutual trust

3. Dialogue makes it possible to share in service to the community

4. Dialogue becomes the medium of authentic witness

Should I take part in dialogue? - This question may be better asked of Christians as 'why not?'. If Christianity is an outward looking faith that seeks to engage with all people, and if Christians understand there to be a *missio Dei,* then in a dialogical encounter Christians can have either an authentic opportunity to share their own faith or have an opportunity to potentially discover something of the work of God in another. The reality is that both may well happen within the dialogue.

Should I look to promote dialogue? – It is naïve to think that that all will enthusiastically endorse the more official forms of dialogue, even if all will participate in the dialogue of life. I well remember the great difficulties in the 1980s for the Revd David Armstrong, then of Limavady Presbyterian Church, when he crossed the road to give a Christmas greeting in the neighbouring Roman Catholic Church. The ensuing 'controversy' of this act of welcome in a politically charged era and region led to the elders of that congregation ultimately dismissing Armstrong as their minister. Yet official sensitivities or reluctance should not allow the numerous forms of dialogical encounter to stall. Leaders need to know how to follow. Dialogue is authentically Christian. It is what Christians do. To do anything less is to be less than fully Christian. That said, within the body of Christ there are many callings. For some in Ireland the challenge of today is to promote and engage in inter-faith issues. The wider Church will not see this as a major priority; that is to be expected. But the Church can empower those with this particular calling to be the vanguard and give a lead to others.

What are the problems with dialogue? - There are forms of dialogue that are not appropriate for Irish Christians to participate in. In a formal dialogue there can be a hidden agenda from one or more participants where the event is used to legitimate a certain, perhaps radical, group, organisation or viewpoint. Coercion can occur when a number of participants 'gang up' on others; manipulation can occur when a conversation or discussion is artificially steered to attempt to create a predetermined outcome. Dialogue has to be open; otherwise it becomes another variation of monologue. In the more formal types of dialogue Christians need to be fully aware of the context within which they are participating. Scripture rightly reminds Christians to be 'shrewd as snakes' (Matthew 10:16) but within this Irish Christians should still positively seek to participate wherever possible. Risk taking is a Christian virtue.

How do I 'do' dialogue? - This can be better answered, as in mission, with an understanding of dialogue as being rather than doing. The principles of dialogue can be lifestyle choices rather than a set of virtues taken up when the time for dialogue somehow arrives. Confining dialogue to formal and official approaches tends to inculcate this false notion. Who a person is should primarily be what they bring to inter-faith encounter and dialogue.

1. Dialogue is the place for conversation that is always 'full of grace' (Colossians 4:6) rather than for clever arguments. Point scoring is not the objective; rather it is the communication of truths that are important to those engaged in the conversation.

2. Dialogue is the place for normal, natural conversation by Christians and others rather than for 'religious' conversation. In 1 Corinthians 13:1-13 Paul extols the virtue of love above everything else. This principle fully applies to any inter-faith encounter. If the Christian 'wins the discussion' but does not overwhelmingly reveal something of God's love in their life then they are only 'a resounding gong or a clashing cymbal' (v1) of which Irish Christianity has had a few down through the years.

3. Dialogue is to be approached with 'gentleness and respect' (1 Peter 3:15) rather than with the intention of showing how clever a participant is. A mutually enriching time will be had when the views of others, and they themselves as individuals, are treated with respect.

4. Dialogue is an encounter rather than a contest. It is a place for fun, learning, sharing, exploring and debate. It is not the place to defend a particular faith perspective but to clarify, enlighten and share. There are no winners or losers. Testimony to God is shared. This is the stuff of life that cannot be reduced to a type of schoolboy 'my side did better than your side' approach. It is both so much greater and so much more important than that.

5. Dialogue is the place for spontaneously sharing who God is to you rather than set speeches. It is more testimony than reasoned argument. There is most certainly a place for careful debate about inter-religious understandings, but that is rarely productive in dialogue. It is more akin to a number of monologues. Being 'prepared to give an answer to everyone who asks you to give a reason for the hope you have' (1 Peter 3:15) is an imaginative, spontaneous and faithful approach. It involves some preparation but that is in the nature of understanding Christian faith and being able to naturally share and show that everywhere, including the inter-faith encounter. Rather than having the politician's knack of giving a set answer

to a question they had not been asked, Christians and other share naturally in dialogue.

6. Dialogue is the place to be open and hopeful rather than defensive. It is entered into with the risk of being converted. Being a Christian today is a risk taking lifestyle, a reverse to the risks associated with not being a conforming Christian under Christendom. The risk of the Christian being converted to another faith or viewpoint in dialogue has to be real if faith is really being shared. The corresponding possibility of someone of another faith becoming a disciple of Christ is equally present and an essential part of authentic dialogue.

7. Dialogue is primarily concerned about the present. The past is not irrelevant but cannot be allowed to dominate. For example, at some point the Irish Sikh community may well be interested to discuss the surprising level of Irish involvement in the terrible massacre of Sikhs at the Golden Temple, Amritsar in 1919, the holiest shrine for Sikhs. A discussion about the role played in the incident by Ireland's Sir Michael O'Dwyer and General JEN Dyer might be useful but cannot be allowed to form the substance of ongoing interaction between Irish Christians and Sikhs. The past, as Ireland knows all too well, is very significant for the present, but it is the past.

8. Dialogue is primarily a meeting of people and their personal religious practices rather than religious philosophies. It is fine for religious scholars to discuss the detailed points of religions in an abstract sense but nobody really believes or follows this abstract, almost neutral, form of faith. It would be possible to distil an abstract understanding of Irish Catholicism but finding someone whose beliefs and practice matched that completely would be a rarity. Faith is lived out by individuals with all the colour and blemishes that life brings. This is the faith that is brought to dialogue and inter-religious encounter. Religious philosophy is not theology, but theology still suffers from the same difficulty in dialogue. Dialogue is a faith encounter, not an abstract discussion. During inter-religious encounter, when participants include several people of the same faith, what becomes apparent very quickly is that they do not have exactly the same faith understanding and practice. Inter-

religious encounter can also be, at times, an internal dialogue. It highlights the need for ongoing intra-religious dialogue. A faith community may have very clearly defined beliefs and practices, but the lived reality will be much more diverse.

What is the Purpose of Dialogue? - Within dialogue there is communication of religious truth in general and, in missional terms, of Christian truth. How do Irish Christians find opportunities to share faith understanding with, say, Irish Jews? Within a dialogical encounter a great deal else happens but Christian truth is certainly shared. This is missional.

At a further level an accurate understanding of the beliefs and practices of others occurs. Given Ireland's relative historic isolation from non-Christian faith communities, there can be a great deal of misinformation about the beliefs and practices of other faiths. There are many ways this is being countered, with education at second and third level making a good impact, but in dialogue it is a believer correcting false understanding rather than an educated outsider. No matter how much understanding the outsider has, there is a level they cannot go beyond. The outsider can know Islamic doctrine, they can describe what happens at Ramadan and its theological significance, but they cannot describe how it feels to complete the Hajj. That can only be shared by an insider, a believer. Dialogue is authentic communication.

There is a significant level of community building involved in dialogue of whatever nature. Friendships are made, misunderstandings overcome and if there are communities with little contact with each other, then dialogue is an essential process in overcoming perceived divisions. People of faith are firstly people of faith before they are Jews, Muslims or Christians. Being a faith full person who happens to be Muslim has something in common with a faith full person who is a Christian that is not shared by a person without religious faith. What such people of faith have in common is always more than creates difference, but Irish history shows that it is the differences that are too often magnified.

Dialogue is mission in that it is engagement with those outside the Christian faith. It is a most helpful and authentically Christian way to engage with people of other faiths, but not the only way.

Inter-Faith Worship and Mission

When Christians worship together they bring a variety of faith understandings that are held together in common affirmations as outlined in the historic creeds and contemporary statements of faith. There are numerous different ways that Christians worship but it is recognisably Christian worship through the object of worship being the Triune God. When Hindus, Muslims and Jews worship, the object of their worship is an understanding of divinity that may, in some cases, be quite close to Christian understanding, and in many other cases be radically different. It is clearly not the same understanding. The implication of this is that when Christians and people of other faith seek to worship together there is a difficulty as the object of the worship must remain undefined beyond some vague 'divine' figure. Even that concept is impossible for Theravada Buddhists (who do not believe in a personal, all powerful God) to maintain. Consequently inter-faith worship is problematic.

The missional importance of this in contemporary Ireland is that there are a number of official inter-faith worship occasions already happening. Many Irish state occasions involve religious figures such as the Catholic and Anglican Archbishops, the Chief Rabbi and more recently an Imam. Under Christendom, in its several Irish varieties, such a situation could never arise as only one recognised religious authority gave legitimation to the secular authority and blessed the state. As post-Christendom has replaced the role of one legitimating religious authority with a number of equally recognised options, Christians cannot 'veto' the involvement of those with whom they have significant religious differences. If Irish Christians feel they cannot participate in such events, then they will simply exclude themselves and life will go on. The state is no longer interested in granting the Church a privileged position. Christians are moving from the point of focus to being one among others. They risk a further relegation to the margins.

There are many other forms of inter-faith worship. Different faith communities can come together and seek to worship together. Christians can be invited to the celebrations and rites of passage of friends from other faiths. Christians can likewise invite friends from other faiths to their important occasions. Christians might invite a religious leader from another faith community to participate in an event and vice versa. In a multi-faith society such occasions, and more, will naturally arise. Christians need to find a way to authentically participate in such a multi-faith nation.

The issue is authentic participation. If Christians simply say no, they exclude themselves from much of the present and future life of Ireland. Some theological understandings will point to this and while such appear to uphold a form of theological integrity, missionally this excludes rather than engages. If Christians simply participate in whatever is happening and invite all and sundry to participate in Christian worship, then authenticity is lost. Some theological elasticity is required but it cannot go beyond breaking point. So, what is the solution?

What is Authentic Inter-Faith Worship? - Irish Christians can authentically participate in inter-faith worship and honour Christ when following a pattern of serial worship. This has developed as best practice for all the faiths involved and needs to be recognised as such. In this form of worship, which might take place in a public or civic occasion, or when two faith communities come together, each faith community develops a shorter act of worship that does not require or expect the involvement of anyone outside that particular faith community. Others who are at the event will respectfully observe the worship of, say, Muslims but neither be invited to join in Muslim prayer or have any expectation that they should do so. When Christians offer their time of worship it is conceived so that there is no complete congregational response needed. Hymns or worship songs are problematic as they are normally for full congregational participation.

A form of serial worship can be a way to allow friends, who follow different faiths, to pray alongside each other and for each other. Because different faiths are followed does not mean that friends can share almost everything in life except for their respective faith understanding and practice.

Inter-faith worship is not something that most Irish Christians will want to rush into. And they are right to be cautious. Even a scant glance at the historic creeds will point to a number of areas of difficulty for a community that declares Jesus to be Saviour and Lord when attempting to worship alongside people who do not. But for missional reasons it is important to find a means by which inter-faith worship can be entered with integrity. Serial worship provides such a means.

Inter-faith Ireland is a reality and is both a necessary and appropriate place for a missional engagement by Ireland's Christians. As Christians in Ireland seek to communicate their faith in meaningful ways to those around them, they need church structures that are appropriate, missional and sustainable. The search for this forms the final chapters of this book.

Questions

1   Is Christianity one way among many or The Way? Why?

2   How can your church work with people from other faith groups?

3   Is an Irish Muslim an Irish person who follows Islam or a Muslim who happens to live in Ireland? What might be the implications of your answer?

Chapter Nine:
Towards an Irish Missional Church

Into the Future

In the days before satellite navigation became commonplace people used to wind down their car window and ask for directions – it almost sounds quaint. I wonder did anyone ever get the proverbial reply of, 'well, if I was going there I wouldn't start from here.' If one was to invent the Christian Church for Ireland in 2010 nobody would start with what we have, nor indeed with the recent history. But there should be confidence that the future can be different and better than the immediate past. There is hope for Ireland in that old denominational links to nationalism and unionism and community identity are being removed. Faith is becoming faith and not an expression of politics or culture. Christianity, through decline as an institution, is escaping from its Christendom past and is being reborn as a movement. So, what might be an authentic model of missional church for Ireland?

Avery Dulles' classic *Models of the Church* considered the Church as Institution; Mystical Communion; Sacrament; Herald; Servant and Community of Disciples. It is a version of this final designation, an addition in his revised edition, which seems most attractive today. Alternatively, John Driver in *Images of the Church in Mission* interpreted the Church as The Way; Sojourners; The Poor; The Kingdom of God; New Creation; New Humanity; The People of God; The Family of God; The Shepherd and the Flock; Salt, Light and a City; A Spiritual House and A Witnessing Community. Dulles concept of the Church was fairly static and showed allegiance to a form of Christendom whereas Driver was intentionally missional. Yet neither quite captures what is needed in post-everything Ireland. A glance at what is happening in British Christianity at present is helpful; while the two contexts are very different there are warnings and pointers from the British experience that need to be heeded in Ireland. In a number of aspects of society Ireland follows or loosely parallels the British experience and the British context provides a sombre example.

In Britain the Anglican Parish system has basically collapsed. The Christendom model of a local church, usually a church related school and a resident priest with a visible and significant role in the community has already gone. Vicars, especially in rural areas, are increasingly looking after a number of congregations while in the towns and cities small numbers of worshippers meet in large buildings with clergy unknown to the wider community. Within this picture the parish churches with very small congregations are largely surviving. Those worshipping are an insignificant, often elderly fragment of society but this is how it has been for a generation and the elderly members are being replaced by more elderly members. While the wider population is largely indifferent, there is no desire to see such traditional faith communities disappear. The well attended evangelical parishes are showing decline. There are still a significant number of large vibrant congregations but they are not quite as robust as they were a decade ago. However, Cathedral congregations are growing. In a postmodern era, which wants spiritual experience without commitment, Cathedral worship where paid choirs and liturgists put on an impressive 'show' is proving increasingly attractive. Christmas attendance overall continues to grow.

The message is bleaker for the traditional Free Churches. Methodism, the United Reformed Church (URC) and the Salvation Army are becoming unsustainable as national denominations. Given the statistical reality their demise, at least as national bodies, will happen. The URC is currently finding it difficult to maintain its national structure while in 2007 Methodism cut its headquarters staff by 35% with many arguing a similar cut will need to be made again in a couple more years. The 'House Churches', new charismatic groupings that arose in the 1980s, are starting to show decline. Pentecostal churches are largely static although this is obviously much better than the rapid decline of most others. A new form of church known as 'Emerging Church', which will be considered later, has received a lot of attention and finance from the traditional denominations but has yet to show any significant return on this investment. The one area of clear growth is in mono cultural churches where members are drawn from a particular ethnic community and are, at present, being significantly boosted by immigration. Such congregations might worship in a, say, African language and follow cultural patterns from the country of origin.

Yet, do not let this picture imply that Christianity is on the way out. While it is in clear decline in Britain, across the world Christianity is significantly growing, is vibrant, diverse, confident and re-evangelising the west. Christianity in Britain is one of the exceptions to the growth of world Christianity.

So what are the potential ways of being and doing church for Ireland (and elsewhere) for today and at least the next generation?

Models of Church for Twenty-first Century Ireland

Cell Church - Many parishes and congregations have established house or home groups in the last generation. People meet for prayer, Bible study and fellowship in each other's homes on a regular basis to supplement involvement with a larger worshipping community on Sunday. Cell church follows part of this pattern but deviates from this as the cell is seen as the ecclesial body to which the individual belongs. The cell gathering may be supplemented by regular or occasional gatherings or celebrations when the members of a number of associated cells come together but the cell is primary.

Among the advantages of this model are low financial costs, as large premises are not needed. Occasional celebrations can take place in hotels and other hired facilities. It is low cost in terms of staffing needs. Pastoral support comes from the group members, relationship is a key feature of Christian living and members are freed from the demands of numerous committees and organisations. Such structures, the hallmark of an institution, are largely redundant. It even starts to sound a little like the early church of Acts 2:42-47. Could it be that the current decline in vocations is God's way of pointing Christians to new forms of church that are not so reliant (or reliant at all) on paid clergy? Much of what is cell church might be inevitable due to clergy shortage, financial difficulties, and the upkeep of large buildings unsuited to contemporary usage and so on. Rather

155

than reading the signs of the times as pointers to a decline from the past, perhaps these signs should be read as a map towards the future.

Multi-Church - In the last couple of generations parishes and congregations have developed a large number of organisations and fellowship groups to cater for children, youth, women, men, musicians, cultural activities and so on. Part of the recent missional challenge has been to attempt to integrate, say, youth into the Sunday worshipping community. The youth group may operate very successfully with leisure activities, worship, and Bible study but it is often a struggle for such young people and the rest of the existing congregation to find ways of worshipping together that accommodate the variety of preferences and approaches.

Multi-church is an attempt to overcome this by simply not attempting any integration. If the youth group is operating successfully and contains, in different forms, the main constituent elements of church, then acknowledge this as church, indeed celebrate it as such and do not attempt what is now a needless translation into another ecclesial body. So within a parish there might be one or more youth churches, a couple of house churches, a children's church, a women's afternoon church, an older people's church and so on. Sunday is an increasingly busy day through work, sporting, cultural and family commitments so why not recognise the group you attend on a Tuesday evening as church, if it meets such criteria? All these churches are in relationship with each other and the Sunday worshipping community can be viewed as the main or parent church but the other forms are still valid.

This is a recognition that in postmodernity not only does one size not fit all; few want the blandness that can result from creating a form of church and worship that accommodates variety by reduction to the lowest common denominator. Congregations have fought interminable battles over change and difference. Why not solve this by recognising the reality that within any larger congregation there are already a number of 'sub-churches' existing through personal choice? Given the smaller size of each part of the 'multi-church', relationships are emphasised and the missional impact multiplied through various congregations. A potential member is offered a menu to choose from rather than a 'take it or leave it' approach.

Café Church - The days of putting on the 'Sunday best' are gone. Many worshippers now dress down on Sunday when compared to most of the rest of the week and this points to a desire to see church as something that is informal, comfortable and relational rather than as a duty to fulfil. Café church is a development of this where church takes place in a coffee shop or restaurant and so the features are relaxed, casual, welcoming, food based and retain few of the traditional elements of church worship. Café church is not putting a few tables into a church hall with insipid coffee and a plain biscuit, and then singing hymns and listening to a sermon. The venue helps determine the form of worship. Café church is intentionally relational and inviting. It has most of the benefits of cell church with the added missional advantage that it can be advertised and is open access in an attractive, familiar but neutral venue, whereas cell church needs a personal invitation to a newcomer.

Many congregations are starting to experiment with a form of this, but too many are going with the chairs in the church hall approach. After a while the novelty wears off and it just becomes hard work. That is not really trying the model. Café church needs a pleasant, dedicated venue where the food and coffee on offer is attractive in themselves. It needs to be a place where the followers of Jesus hang out with each other in a way that is natural rather than artificial.

Network Church - During Christendom there was one local church in a defined geographical community. Any more than this meant either redrawing the parish boundaries or attempting to thwart the rival or alternative. With the rise of the Protestant denominations society has become used to various alternatives on offer but most congregations still see their 'target' community as geographically defined. Within a town there might be ten or more different denominations but each usually looked on the whole town as their catchment area. While this was the norm there have been exceptions. During the western Protestant missionary expansion of the nineteenth and early twentieth century, in certain areas mission societies recognised that working co-operatively meant that they should keep to certain defined areas and so parts of, for example, Nigeria were, for a couple of generations at least, largely Methodist while neighbouring areas were largely Baptist or Anglican.

Network church is an attempt to recognise that in postmodernity a parish or community need not be defined geographically. Particularly in urban areas people have relatively little in common with those around whom they live, and much more in common with people they interact with in other ways. Via the internet, many now keep in almost daily contact with a bewildering number of people across the world, and yet may very rarely speak to their next door neighbour. Such is the world. There is little point in bemoaning the passing of communities where everyone knew each other and family roots went back generations. For most people that way of life ended with their grandparents and while what has replaced that may be deficient in many ways, it is the reality. Today increasingly few remain in the same area in which they grew up (and that is often now several locations) and if they do remain most of their peers have moved on.

Somebody who works in a city centre office may meet up with those in their own or similar offices in the evening before going home on what is often a time consuming commute. They have a lot in common with those of similar occupation, income, interests and lifestyle. Those they live close to might well be very different in all these categories and so friendships in real or virtual senses increasingly tend to be formed across networks rather than geography.

So what does network church look like? Four Christian friends who live widely apart but work in the town or city centre meet up in a pub or restaurant every Tuesday evening before they go their separate ways. They start to recognise what they are doing is church and the group with whom they associate with on a Sunday but have relatively little in common with is less and less meaningful to them. The recognition that this Tuesday (or whatever day) group has become their church enables them to be more intentional about the level of fellowship, pastoral care and Bible study with which they engage. Network church shares many of the advantages of cell church but is not geographically defined. Its missional significance is that the four friends, who are friends perhaps through working in the same industry, are each in contact with a wider network of colleagues and those in similar occupations. Through their wider friendships occasionally another is invited to join their small group. Most will drop away but occasionally one will 'stick', learn what Christian faith and Christian community is about and become a disciple.

Alt.worship - Developing different worship styles has been a normal part of Christianity and alt.worship is such a development that focuses on new, often contemplative worship experiences. Rather than following a charismatic direction this will delve into the past and seek resources from the early church, the monastic orders, medieval Christianity, the Orthodox tradition and so on. It is a postmodern, eclectic approach to worship that combines historic approaches with contemporary media such as film, sound, touch and image to create a worship experience that seeks to contemporise a historic faith that can be owned by more than one tradition. In most forms of worship, be they traditional or charismatic, the congregation is told what to do and is expected to respond in a uniform way within a liturgy or as guided by a leader. In alt.worship there is a much more individualistic approach where a variety of worship experiences, using several different media, are happening simultaneously and individuals interact with what they wish when they want.

Rather than a particular model of church this is better seen as a particular model of worship. Yet there are some who will choose this, perhaps, monthly approach as their only form of Christian worship and by default it is their church.

Dispersed Monastic Community - While many Catholic orders have seen their vocations almost cease recently the whole idea of monasticism has become more appealing to a new generation, including many Protestants. Rather than belonging to a local church with the mixture of people, worship styles, spiritual experience and so on, a small number want to identify with like-minded Christians in a disciplined form of

Christian worship, life and fellowship. The limitations of geography are overcome by each committing to follow a similar pattern of worship and fellowship individually but recognising they are participating, in a dispersed way, among a group that share the same approach and understanding. So at the same time each morning the members of this dispersed community may be found following the same liturgy and living out a rule of life, albeit one that stops short of vows of poverty, chastity and obedience.

The Northumbria Community (www.northumbriacommunity.org) is one such group. A daily office reflecting Celtic Christian spirituality is shared by the community members at three set times per day with resources made available through their web site supporting this ecumenical group. There are monthly regional gatherings which many, but not all, members participate in. It combines the commitment of a monastic community with the freedom of a 'normal' personal life. While there is an element of withdrawal from the challenges of participating in a parish church, for most members of this dispersed monastic community the rule of life is taken in addition to their membership of a local church.

Emerging Church - A form of church that combines many of the elements of the models above, and that has been receiving a great deal of attention in Britain and North America is what is known as 'Emerging Church'. There are examples that display certain characteristics more clearly than others but this form of church is largely urban, is focused on relationships, is loosely configured in terms of leadership and membership, uses alt.worship styles, is often related to the club scene and usually appeals to younger, well educated people. It stresses the importance of community but that defined by network more than geography, is inclusive, is not particularly charismatic, does not need clergy, significant finance or its own premises, and is intentionally small and not obsessed with propositional truth. It is participatory therefore active rather than passive, artistic and experimental and has no intention of building a faith community that needs to be in the same place and keep the same form and worship style for any significant length of time.

Beyond this it is hard to be more definitive. It is a thoroughly postmodern expression of Christianity and as such defies categorisation. It varies according to the tastes of its membership and appeals both to those who are disenchanted with traditional forms of church and those for whom church is an alien culture but for whom this 'emerging' community is more recognisable to their usually urban lifestyle.

Despite gaining a lot of attention in Britain, such emerging churches have yet to make much missional impact. At present most operate more as 'survivors' groups, helping those disillusioned with institutional Christianity to find a form of church they can participate in, one that allows questions without having to give definitive answers. Such 'survivors' groups are very important to address the drift away from Christianity but have yet to show that they are able to missionally engage with those without a Christian background.

There are many attractions with a number of these alternative models. Inherited or traditional church is failing overall and not just individual congregations, although many Christians are only starting to recognise this. To make a missional impact different forms of church are needed, indeed for the Church itself to have a future requires a radical change. These models allow for individualism and personal choice, are designed to appeal to postmodern society and to minimise the aspects of Christian community that many find difficult. In short, they contain aspects of indulgent Christianity that cater to the wishes and sensibilities of contemporary society, are attractive and may well be missionally effective.

Of course, seeing indulgent Christianity as a positive is very problematic. There are elements within most of these models of church that deny aspects of the good news of Jesus Christ. Yet there is much within inherited church that also denies aspects of the gospel and so I am not arguing for a move from a good place in a problematic direction. Current church is problematic, it is already largely broken and so an alternative, even with flaws, may still offer helpful possibilities.

Other problems with many of these models are that most are applicable to individuals rather than families. The Christian nurture of children is not well catered for. With the decline in Christian involvement in education the prime place for Christian nurture and teaching will need to be the home rather the school or even parish or congregation. But even this admission shows part of the appeal of new forms of church in the present and future. Family itself is breaking down. Ireland is catching up the rest of the western world for divorce rate and over a third of all Irish births already occur outside marriage. A model of church that focuses on the traditional family as the ideal and the norm is in itself becoming irrelevant in contemporary Ireland. That is not to argue for a change in how Christians view the importance of marriage. It is simply recognising that to make a missional impact in the Ireland of the present, having a starry eyed idealistic image of society is not helpful. The content of the good news does not change, but the way Christian community is expressed must constantly evolve.

One potential model that should be denied as authentically church is 'virtual church'. Logging on to a site that provides email prayers, podcast sermons and downloadable worship from the comfort of your own armchair can be helpful but cannot be in itself authentic Christian community. While web based approaches can offer much to support contemporary expressions of church, a form of Christian community that intentionally avoids the need to physically meet has to be a denial of the incarnation. That appears to take indulgence one step too far. St Pixels (www.stpixels.com) is one example of how such a project has many helpful possibilities and missional advantages, particularly as a taster of Christian community, but it cannot be the sole form of church for those for whom there are other alternatives.

Much of this thinking comes easier to those from a Protestant background who are used to a context of religious plurality, a 'choose what you like' approach and a stress on the individual over the community. For Catholics there is a much greater leap of imagination required but part of that journey has already been made. Catholics are increasingly becoming used to different 'types' of worship and so Saturday evening might be a 'folk mass', Sunday afternoon a Polish language mass, Sunday night a 'youth mass', there might be an additional Irish language mass or even the offer of the recently restored Tridentine mass. Within a parish there may be a variety of groups such as a charismatic prayer group, the Legion of Mary, St Vincent de Paul and so on. There is choice within a parish or area and some of the models detailed above are a development of what can already be conceived rather than a radical departure.

I have outlined a number of possibilities each of which already has existing, viable examples. Just how I imagine the future Irish church to be forms the substance of the final chapter.

Questions

1   Which model best describes your church?

2   Which model do you find most attractive? Why?

3   Which model do you think might be attractive to those you know who are not regular worshippers? Why?

Chapter Ten:

The Future Church in Ireland

In this final chapter I am deliberately seeking, if not to be controversial, at least to state my case to an extreme. This is to provoke reflection and action. The future may be nothing like this, the institutional form of Irish Christianity may revive and flourish, but I do not think so. If I overstate the case and the argument leads to urgent thought and response, then such an approach has been well worth while.

What is an appropriate and sustainable missional model of church for Ireland? It is the argument of this book that traditional, institutional or inherited church, including the varieties of Pentecostal and even African based congregations that have seen significant growth in recent years, will struggle to continue in an institutional sense in Ireland beyond another twenty or thirty years. Where they continue to survive there will be little missional impact. Some individual congregations will continue but overall inherited church will struggle to survive. It is also the argument here that much of this is good news in that it allows Irish Christianity to escape from its Christendom(s) past and become more authentically the movement of the followers of Jesus. Yet there needs to be some structure to help define community. 'Liquid Church' where almost anything is appropriate as long as it works for some is an attractive concept for postmodernity but to avoid defining an appropriate and authentically missional ecclesial body is to just escape the consequences of the issue. Community involves boundaries. Whether the 'rules' that govern behaviour and interaction are explicit or implicit is immaterial. Such conventions are needed and here I seek to suggest what might be a helpful approach. A fluid rather than rigid model is needed that takes into account postmodernity and Ireland's particular post-Christendom legacy. It needs to require less finance and clergy involvement than alternatives and be effectively missional rather than primarily pastoral given the Ireland of today.

Here I am primarily talking about local congregations. The denominations as national structures will change in that

Catholicism will remain as a national church with a national institutional structure, albeit much slimmed down. The Church of Ireland will be unable to staff and finance a large number of its congregations, particularly in the Republic of Ireland and while it will continue in an institutional sense it will only be enabled to do this by its merging (or effectively taking over) one of more other denominations. Without this the Church of Ireland will struggle to justify any claim to be a national Church. Several of the other Protestant denominations will merge, with the Anglicans or with each other, primarily to rationalise their resources. Such rationalisation between the Anglicans and Methodists and between the Methodists and Presbyterians has been happening in a very limited way for a couple of generations and the pace and scope of this will increase and involve new partners. Some small denominations will basically disappear. There is most unlikely to be one united Protestant Church in Ireland. Given the perceived theological differences between the various strands of the Irish Protestant family such agreement, even when faced with oblivion, is unlikely to be found. Some will prefer to view themselves as the 'righteous remnant' heading into the desert rather than 'compromise' core beliefs and practices.

There will continue to be a number of congregations that look very similar to many that currently exists. People will still turn up to listen passively to a preacher, sing hymns, pay their way and go home again. However this will make no missional impact in the community. It will be not unlike the Masonic Order – a gathering of apparently normal people who every now and again do this strange ritual that nobody else understands and that seems, frankly, bizarre.

At best there will be 'hospice churches'. These are congregations that do not have the energy or desire to change. They recognise they have no future but continue to exist so that their members may continue to worship and live out their Christian lives in ways that are familiar and helpful to them and clergy will offer what amounts to palliative pastoral care. Many existing congregations are already this. This is not a 'bad' form of church, indeed a lot of effort should go into maintaining the structures of buildings, finance and clergy for this 'hospice church' movement to exist for the twenty or thirty years it is needed. But it must be recognised that this form of church will not be missionally effective. Church attendance trends tell us this already. It is just too divorced from what Ireland has already become. An occasional person will join and come to faith. God is sovereign and anything is possible. But overall such church will not work missionally.

It is easy to critique and much harder to point to the solution. So, what do I think the missional local congregation of the future will look like?

The Necessary Missional Church in Ireland

Each individual congregation in Ireland of the (near) future will be small. A membership of between eight and sixteen people will be the norm. This allows for deep relationships to develop and for pastoral support to be mutual, rather than requiring paid professional staff. A membership of at least eight allows for variety and support and a viable community given the increasing inability to find mutually convenient meeting times for a large group. Less than sixteen encourages a full participation by all and recognises the significance of each individual within the church. More than sixteen allows an unhelpful passivity, so apparent in most contemporary congregations, to develop. Of course, eight and sixteen are not prescriptive numbers but indicative of the approximate size. Given the numerical strength within many Catholic parishes this number may seem extremely small. It does not mean that in an existing parish there will only be a dozen worshippers left. Rather the large parish has subdivided into a number of small units. Within this size the character of the missional church of the future will be as follows:

1. The church in Ireland of the (near) future will meet in the homes of its members, or in local facilities such as hotels. These meeting places will require little finance, will be comfortable and inviting and allow a relational rather than formal Christianity to develop.

2. The church in Ireland of the (near) future will not have paid clergy. There is no need for such as pastoral care and Christian teaching will be mutual. This Christianity will be supported by an

167

enhanced and refocused network of monasteries and colleges that are primarily mission resource centres. It is to such places that local leaders will go to equip themselves with the task of understanding their faith and the community around them sufficiently to engage in appropriate mission and evangelisation. Christians will pay to attend these professionally delivered courses that will finance these centres. Since Christians do not have to significantly finance their local church expression such finance is available for training courses and other mission activities. It is in these monasteries and colleges where the nationally recognised leaders of Christianity will be found; a return to the Celtic Abbots rather than the Roman Bishops.

3. The church in Ireland of the (near) future will normally meet in these small groups and understand each to be a self-contained ecclesial community but will also see the need to join with other such groups in celebratory events centred around the Christian festivals such as Easter, Pentecost and Christmas. An increasing number of these celebrations will take place in public spaces in towns and cities, and in places of traditional Christian pilgrimage. The sacrament of Holy Communion will be less significant but increasingly led by what used to be called lay people who are either authorised by their own community for this role or use elements that have previously been consecrated. It may be that the celebratory events have a sacramental dimension but more normally this will happen in the small community.

4. The church in Ireland of the (near) future will require very little finance to support its life but will still require a significant financial commitment from its mature members to support mission activities that will be undertaken by orders and parachurch agencies. There will be other expenses for the resources each will use to help sustain their spiritual development and training programmes. Enthusiastic and capable Christians seeking to follow a vocational life will find opportunities to serve in these mission agencies rather than in parish based roles. God will still call men and women into paid, full time service but these will be almost exclusively missional appointments.

5. The church in Ireland of the (near) future will be missional in all that it does. Each local ecclesial community will understand its role to attract new people to its community and make disciples. Once the figure of around sixteen or thereabouts is reached the group will subdivide and form two new and distinct ecclesial bodies.

6. The church in Ireland of the (near) future will meet on Sunday and every other day. Given twenty-first century lifestyles and postmodern choices each community will find the appropriate days and times when they come together and there will be an infinite variety regarding time, duration and frequency.

7. The church in Ireland of the (near) future will be based in locations that are not necessarily related to where people live. Increasingly churches will be formed of people who have something in common such as occupation or recreation. A church might meet a couple of evenings a week in a city centre restaurant as all its members work in the city but live (or more accurately sleep) widely dispersed across the city. Another church might meet close by the local school where the church members are employed. There will be an infinite variety of expression of church.

8. The church in Ireland of the (near) future will not plan to be present in its current location and form in a long-term way. It will seek to replicate itself and so sustain the Christian life and witness but as it exists in a very fluid world any attempt to build itself a permanent existence in one expression is doomed to failure, as recent Irish Christian history has demonstrated. The Christian movement as a truly pilgrim people will be rediscovered.

9. The church in Ireland of the (near) future will not follow a similar pattern of community worship. Each church will contain worship, Bible study, discipleship, sacraments and mission but how this is carried out will differ radically. Some churches will concentrate on certain aspects more than others. That may be the main reason why an individual associates with a certain church. A typical meeting will be impossible to describe. Some gatherings will emphasise Bible study or worship, other occasions will more resemble social gatherings. The distinction will not be important. Each church, in order to be a church, will

need core Christian activities bur each will express this in an individual way.

This is deliberately not a 'ten point plan'. Such a neat typology implies that transitioning to this church of the (near) future is a managerial task that will be successful through following the right methods. My list above is a description of virtues and qualities rather than things to do. In the complicated, fluid, messy world of today and tomorrow there are fuzzy edges everywhere. We may long for clear definition but such no longer exists. Institutions have boundaries, clear directives, obvious management lines and accepted ways of operating. The church of the near future, as it exists in a postmodern world, will have a form of structure but none of the sharp edges Christians have been used to and found surprisingly comfortable. Some might long for the past but it is the past. The future is never clear but as a movement Christianity is better equipped to enter the unknown.

The institution that is Christianity is collapsing in Ireland and its future, I consider, is not uncertain as its demise is assured. But there is a wonderful future for the movement called Christianity. Irish Christians are called to recognise this change and develop forms of Christianity that are sustainable, appropriate, missional and authentically related to Jesus. It is not often that a 1500 year old institution is given the opportunity to reinvent itself. Such is the opportunity in Ireland today. Led by the Spirit, Irish Christians, like those Celtic evangelists who put their fragile boats into the Atlantic with little idea if or where they would land, can still be confident that God is with us. Let us journey where God is leading with hope, excitement and total uncertainty.

Questions

1   What is your reaction to this future scenario?

2   What, for you, are the flaws with this model?

3   How do you conceive the future church in Ireland?

Select Bibliography

Stephen Bevans & Roger Schroeder
Constants in Context: A Theology of Mission for Today
(Maryknoll, NY: Orbis, 2004)

Michael Boss & Eamon Maher (eds)
Engaging Modernity (Dublin: Veritas, 2003)

David Carnduff
Ireland's Lost Heritage (Antrim: IPBC, 2003)

Richard Clarke
A Whisper of God (Dublin: Columba, 2006)

Niall Coll & Paschal Scallon (eds)
A Church with a Future (Dublin: Columba, 2005)

Donal Dorr
Mission in Today's World (Dublin: Columba, 2000)

John Drane
Do Christians Know How to be Spiritual? (Oxford: DLT, 2005)

John Driver
Images of the Church in Mission
(Scottdale, PA: Herald, 1997)

Avery Dulles
Models of the Church (London: Bantam, 1991)

Robert Dunlop
Evangelicals in Ireland (Dublin: Columba, 2004)

Marianne Elliott
The Catholics of Ulster (New York: Basic Books, 2001)

Ian Ellis
Vision and Reality: A Survey of Twentieth Century Irish Inter-Church Attitudes (Belfast: IIS-QUB, 1992)

Ajith Fernando
Acts: The NIV Application Commentary
(Grand Rapids: Zondervan, 1998)

RF Foster
Luck and the Irish (London: Penguin, 2007)

Louise Fuller
Irish Catholicism Since 1950: The Undoing of a Culture
(Dublin: Gill & Macmillan, 2004)

Louise Fuller (ed)
Irish and Catholic (Dublin: Columba, 2006)

Tom Garvin
Preventing the Future (Dublin: Gill & Macmillan, 2005)

Paul Heelas & Linda Woodhead
The Spiritual Revolution (Oxford: Blackwell, 2005)

Tom Inglis
Moral Monopoly (Dublin: UCD Press, 1998)

Glenn Jordan
*Not of This World: Evangelical Protestants in Northern
Ireland* (Belfast: Blackstaff, 2001)

Mary Kenny
Goodbye to Catholic Ireland (Dublin: New Island, 2000)

Andrew Kirk
What is Mission (Oxford: DLT, 1999)
Mission Under Scrutiny (Oxford: DLT, 2006)

Joseph Liechty & Cecilia Clegg
Moving Beyond Sectarianism (Dublin: Columba, 2001)

Caitriona McClean
Moving On? Catholic Ministry in Ireland
(Liskeard: Exposure, 2006)

Moira McCombe & MM Khan
Muslims in Northern Ireland (Belfast: Al-Nisa Association, 2005)

Alister McGrath
The Future of Christianity (Oxford: Blackwell, 2002)

David McWilliams
The Pope's Children (Dublin: Gill & Macmillan, 2006)
The Generation Game (Dublin: Gill & Macmillan, 2007)

Claire Mitchell
Religion, Identity and Politics in Northern Ireland:
(Aldershot: Ashgate, 2006)

Stuart Murray
Post-Christendom: Church and Mission in a Strange New World (Milton Keynes: Paternoster, 2004)
Church After Christendom
(Milton Keynes: Paternoster, 2004)

Lesslie Newbiggin
The Gospel in a Pluralist Society (London: SPCK, 1989)

Fran Porter
Changing Women, Changing Worlds: Evangelical Women in Church, Community and Politics (Belfast: Blackstaff, 2001)
Faith in a Plural Society (Belfast: CCCI, 2008)

Norman Richardson (ed)
A Tapestry of Beliefs: Christian Traditions in Northern Ireland (Belfast: Blackstaff, 1998)

Stephen Skuce
The Faiths of Ireland (Dublin: Columba, 2006)

David Smith
Mission After Christendom (London: DLT, 2003)

Bryan Stone
Evangelism after Christendom (Nashville, TN: Brazos, 2007)

Norman Taggart
Conflict, Controversy and Co-Operation: The Irish Council of Churches and 'The Troubles' 1968-1972
(Dublin: Columba, 2004)

Vinvent Twomey
The End of Irish Catholicism? (Dublin: Veritas, 2003)

JR Walsh
Religion: The Irish Experience (Dublin: Veritas, 2003)

Pete Ward
Liquid Church (Carlisle: Paternoster, 2002)

Chris Wright
The Mission of God (Leicester: IVP, 2006)

Department of Theological Questions, Irish Inter-Church Meeting
Being Church in the New Millennium (Dublin: Veritas, 2000)

Web Resources

www.alternativeworship.org/

www.cafechurch.org.au/

www.celluk.org.uk

www.ecocongregationireland.org

www.northumbriacommunity.org

www.prayerfoundation.org/virtual_monastery.htm

www.sanctus1.co.uk/

www.simplechurch.co.uk

www.stpixels.com